Muscular Dystrophy

DISEASES & DISORDERS

Muscular Dystrophy

Melissa Abramovitz

LUCENT BOOKS
A part of Gale, Cengage Learning

GALE
CENGAGE Learning

Detroit • New York • San Francisco • New Haven, Conn • Waterville, Maine • London

LIBRARY OF CONGRESS CATALOGING-IN-PUBLICATION DATA

Abramovitz, Melissa, 1954-
  Muscular dystrophy / by Melissa Abramovitz.
    p. cm. – (Diseases and disorders)
  Includes bibliographical references and index.
  ISBN 978-1-4205-0073-8 (hardcover)
  1. Muscular dystrophy–Juvenile literature. I. Title.
  RC935.M7A27 2008
  616.7'48–dc22

                                            2008013343

Lucent Books
27500 Drake Rd
Farmington Hills MI 48331

ISBN-13: 978-1-4205-0073-8
ISBN-10: 1-4205-0073-2

Printed in the United States of America
2 3 4 5 6 7 12 11 10 09 08

Table of Contents

"The Most Difficult Puzzles Ever Devised"

Charles Best, one of the pioneers in the search for a cure for diabetes, once explained what intrigued him so about medical research: "It's not just the gratification of knowing one is helping people," he confided, "although that probably is a more heroic and selfless motivation. Those feelings may enter in, but truly, what I find best is the feeling of going toe to toe with nature, of trying to solve the most difficult puzzles ever devised. The answers are there somewhere, those keys that will solve the puzzle and make the patient well. But how will those keys be found?"

Since the dawn of civilization, nothing has so puzzled people—and often frightened them, as well—as the onset of illness in a body or mind that seemed healthy before. Being unable to reverse conditions such as a seizure, the inability of a heart to pump, or the sudden deterioration of muscle tone in a small child, or even to understand why they occur was unspeakably frustrating to healers. Even before there were names for such conditions, before they were understood at all, each was a reminder of how complex the human body was and how vulnerable.

While our grappling with understanding diseases has been frustrating at times, it has also provided some of humankind's most heroic accomplishments. Alexander Fleming's accidental discovery in 1928 of a mold that could be turned into penicillin has resulted in the saving of untold millions of lives. The isolation of the enzyme insulin has reversed what was once a death sentence for anyone with diabetes. There also have been great strides in combating conditions for which there is not yet a cure. Medicines can help AIDS patients live longer, diagnostic tools such as mammography and ultrasounds can help doctors find tumors while they are treatable, and laser surgery techniques have made the most intricate, minute operations routine.

This "toe-to-toe" competition with diseases and disorders is even more remarkable when viewed in a historical continuum. An astonishing amount of progress has been made in a very short time. Just two hundred years ago, the existence of germs as a cause of some diseases was unknown. In fact, less than 150 years ago a British surgeon named Joseph Lister had difficulty persuading his fellow doctors that washing their hands before delivering a baby might increase the chances of a healthy delivery (especially if they had just attended to a diseased patient)!

Each book in Lucent's Diseases and Disorders series explores a disease or disorder and the knowledge that has been accumulated (or discarded) by doctors through the years. Each book also examines the tools used for pinpointing a diagnosis, as well as the various means that are used to treat or cure a disease. Finally, new ideas are presented—techniques or medicines that may be on the horizon.

Frustration and disappointment are still part of medicine because not every disease or condition can be cured or prevented. But the limitations of knowledge are constantly being pushed outward; the "most difficult puzzles ever devised" are finding challengers every day.

Jerry Lewis and the Muscular Dystrophy Association Telethon

When many people think of muscular dystrophy, they automatically think of the annual Jerry Lewis Muscular Dystrophy Association (MDA) Telethon that takes place on Labor Day weekend. The telethon has raised over a billion dollars for patient services and research on a group of diseases called the muscular dystrophies and has dramatically increased public awareness of these devastating illnesses. The telethon has been held since 1966.

Before the event became a nationally broadcast phenomenon, actor and comedian Jerry Lewis began hosting local four-hour telethons in 1952 in New York City to benefit the Muscular Dystrophy Associations of America (now called the MDA). He committed himself to these telethons after a member of the staff on *Colgate Comedy Hour*, a television show featuring Lewis and entertainer Dean Martin, asked Lewis to help with muscular dystrophy fundraising. After the local telethons were successful for several years, the Muscular Dystrophy Associations of America approached Lewis about hosting a bigger, longer event. He agreed, and it was scheduled for Labor Day weekend in 1966. Many people expected the nineteen-hour telethon

Entertainer Jerry Lewis, left, poses with Sarah Schwegel, one of the many children with muscular dystrophy who have appeared on the annual Muscular Dystrophy Association Telethon, which Lewis began hosting as a local event in 1952. The telethon has raised over $1 billion for patient services and research.

to fail because a lot of folks were out of town for the holiday weekend, but it was a smashing success and raised over one million dollars. Many celebrities helped Lewis by entertaining viewers and speaking out for muscular dystrophy research.

By 1968, word had spread about the telethon's success, and MDA created the Love Network, a group of television stations that aired the telethon. The Love Network began with four stations, and by 2007 one hundred ninety Love Network stations broadcast the telethon, which is now held in Las Vegas and lasts for over twenty-one hours. In 2007, the telethon raised over sixty-three million dollars. Jerry Lewis continues to be involved with year-round planning of the telethon, and he now hosts the first five and last five hours of the annual event, with co-hosts and entertainers filling in for the rest of the time. "Jerry's kids" (the many children and teens affected by muscular dystrophy) and their families continue to appear on the show to tell their stories.

According to the MDA:

> No one knows why Jerry Lewis, MDA's number one volunteer, chooses to devote so much time to helping people with neuromuscular diseases [diseases that affect the nerves and muscles]. He feels it isn't important why he's involved, rather, it's important that he's involved . . . Despite battling debilitating pulmonary fibrosis [lung disease], severe back pain and a heart attack in recent years, the MDA National Chairman has never missed a Telethon.[1]

The Importance of the Telethon

The funds raised by the telethon are critical for providing services and sponsoring research to help more than 250,000 Americans who have some form of muscular dystrophy. In addition, MDA funds worldwide research that aims to help the millions throughout the world who are affected. The muscular dystrophies affect children, teenagers, and adults of all ages, causing varying degrees of disability and often leading to early death. There is no cure for any of these diseases, and available treatments do not significantly slow the course of the illnesses.

MDA has established 225 hospital-affiliated clinics that provide diagnostic services and ongoing care to thousands of patients in the United States. MDA also pays for more than four thousand children to go to MDA summer camps each year. "Each year MDA supports nearly 90 summer camps across the country. MDA Camp is a magical place where year-round skills are developed and where a child with a disability can just be a kid,"[2] says the MDA.

MDA also helps patients buy and repair wheelchairs, leg braces, and special communication devices. They provide

Jerry Lewis stands before a tote board that tracks the contributions and pledges received at the annual Muscular Dystrophy Association Telethon.

free flu shots to patients and sponsor over two hundred local offices that conduct educational seminars and support groups for patients and families. MDA publishes magazines, brochures, videos, books, and a web site to educate those affected by muscular dystrophy and the general public. These services and MDA's research support would not be possible without the telethon.

Another Perspective

Over the years Jerry Lewis has received numerous awards for his volunteer work on behalf of muscular dystrophy, including a nomination in 1977 for the Nobel Peace Prize. When he nominated Lewis, Wisconsin congressional representative Les Aspin said, "Jerry Lewis is a man for all seasons, all people, all times. His name has, in the hearts of millions, become synonymous with peace, love, and brotherhood."[3]

Even with all the accolades, however, some advocates for the disabled criticize Lewis. They claim he has made disabled people into objects of pity. In one *New York Times* interview in 1992, muscular dystrophy patient Evan J. Kemp Jr., then chair of the government's Equal Opportunity Commission, said about the telethon, "I have always had problems with the pity approach to raising money. I think emotions can be turned on without pity stories."[4]

Disabled people have also led many demonstrations calling for the end of the telethon. Mike Ervin, who was a Muscular Dystrophy Association poster child in the 1960s, later became an outspoken critic of the telethon. He cofounded a group called Jerry's Orphans to protest against Lewis. Ervin appeared in a documentary film called "The Kids Are All Right" to raise awareness of the issue. His philosophy is explained on a web site promoting the film:

> The telethon routinely implies that the source of the problems people with disabilities face is their medical conditions and the answer to their problems is curing them. Millions of viewers tune in every year and come

away with the idea that people with disabilities need pity and charity rather than accessible public transportation and housing, employment opportunities and other civil rights that a democratic society should ensure for all its citizens.[5]

Despite the criticisms and protests, the MDA Telethon continues year after year in hopes of making life better for people with muscular dystrophy. As the MDA states, "Until there's a cure . . . There's a Telethon."[6]

CHAPTER ONE

What Is Muscular Dystrophy?

Muscular dystrophy (MD) is a group of disorders that weaken muscles in the body, including those that make the body move and others that control certain internal organs. The word dystrophy comes from the Greek words "dys," meaning abnormal, and "trophe," which means nourishment. Muscular dystrophy means that the nourishment of muscles is defective. This is not to say that the affected person does not eat a diet that provides ideal nourishment to the muscles, but rather that the muscles become wasted and weak due to other factors such as deficiencies of certain proteins in muscle tissue.

The muscle weakness is progressive, meaning that it gets worse over time. The rate of progression varies among individuals and with particular types of MD. The weakness also affects both sides of the body in most cases; that is, if one arm is weak, the other arm will also be weak. Doctors refer to this as being symmetrical. People are born with MD, though some do not show signs until childhood, adolescence, or adulthood.

How Muscles Work

The body has different types of muscles: voluntary muscles, heart muscles, and smooth muscles. The human body contains 434 voluntary muscles, also known as skeletal muscles. These muscles are under voluntary control, meaning that people move them by contracting or relaxing them at will. Heart

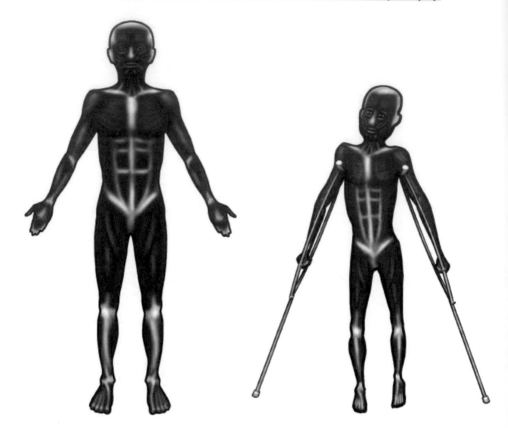

Normal, healthy musculature   **Muscular dystrophy**

A drawing of the musculature of a person with muscular dystrophy
(right) shows how the disease leaves muscles weak and wasted,
as compared to the muscles of someone with normal, healthy
musculature (left).

and smooth muscles are involuntary, meaning they work without people having to consciously think about them or control
their motion. For example, the lungs expand and contract even
when one is not thinking about breathing. Heart muscle con-
trols the function of the heart, and smooth muscles are found in
the gastrointestinal system, blood vessels, lungs, bladder, and
reproductive tract. Muscular dystrophy primarily involves voluntary muscles, though it can also affect the heart and smooth
muscles.

When a person has a disease like muscular dystrophy, their muscles lose the ability to contract and relax and begin to get weak. When this happens, voluntary muscles can no longer pull on bones and joints to make them move and heart and smooth

---

Sir Charles Bell

Sir Charles Bell was born in Edinburgh, Scotland, in 1774. A brilliant student and talented artist, he began studying medicine at the University of Edinburgh after finishing high school. While still a student at the university, he started teaching anatomy classes and writing and illustrating a book on human anatomy under the guidance of his older brother, John, who was a professor and doctor. After Charles graduated, he attended the Royal College of Surgeons and became an outstanding specialist in surgery, anatomy, and the study of the nervous system.

Charles moved to London in 1804 and continued to write and illustrate medical textbooks, work as a surgeon, teach, and conduct research on nerves. In 1831 he was knighted by King George IV in honor of his achievements.

In 1836 he returned to his beloved homeland of Scotland and died there in 1842. Besides being remembered as the doctor who wrote the first formal description of muscular dystrophy, his name is attached to several neurological phenomena including Bell's Palsy, Bell's Law, Bell's Nerve, Bell's Spasm, and Bell-Magendie Law.

British anatomist Sir Charles Bell is credited with writing the first formal description of muscular dystrophy.

muscles cannot perform other functions such as pumping blood, filling the lungs with air, or moving food through the digestive system. Depending on which muscles are affected, muscle weakness can prevent an individual with muscular dystrophy from doing things such as walking, eating, or breathing.

Weakened muscles become inactive, which in turn leads them to shrink and break down. This is known as atrophy. When some muscles atrophy, fat and connective tissue may replace muscle tissue, so the muscles appear to be enlarged, but they are still very weak because these other types of cells cannot perform the functions of muscles. Sometimes weakened muscles also become tightened, a condition called a contracture. Contractures can be very painful and can make muscles even more difficult to move.

Identifying Muscular Dystrophy

Muscular dystrophy was first described in 1830 by the Scottish surgeon Sir Charles Bell. According to the National Institute of Neurological Disorders and Stroke:

> Sir Charles Bell wrote an essay about an illness that caused progressive weakness in boys. Six years later, another scientist reported on two brothers who developed generalized weakness, muscle damage, and replacement of damaged muscle tissue with fat and connective tissue. At that time the symptoms were thought to be signs of tuberculosis [a serious infection of the lungs]. In the 1850's, descriptions of boys who grew progressively weaker, lost the ability to walk, and died at an early age became prominent in medical journals . . . It soon became evident that the disease had more than one form, and that these diseases affected people of either sex and of all ages.[7]

Doctors have identified nine major forms of MD. Some of the major forms have several subtypes. Each weakens different muscle groups, starts at different ages, and has a different prognosis, or expected outcome. The National Institute of Neurological Disorders and Stroke explains: "Some cases may be mild and progress very slowly over a normal lifespan, while others produce severe muscle weakness, functional disability, and loss of the ability to walk. Some children with MD die in infancy while others live into adulthood with only moderate disability."[8]

Duchenne Muscular Dystrophy

The most common form of muscular dystrophy is Duchenne muscular dystrophy (DMD). This disorder is named after

French neurologist Guillame Benjamin Armand Duchenne, top, holds an electrode to a patient's head. The most common form of muscular dystrophy is named after Duchenne, who conducted important research on the disease.

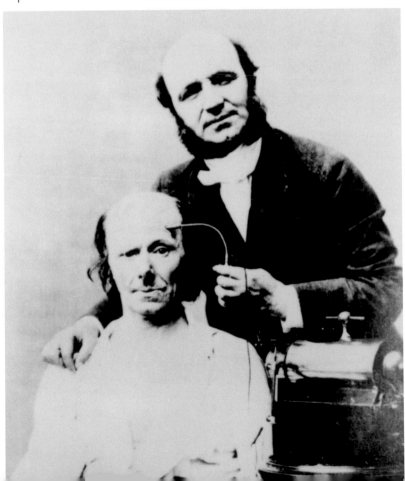

the French neurologist Guillame Benjamin Amand Duchenne, who first described it in his book *De L'electrisation Localisée* in 1861. Recent historical evidence suggests that the English doctor Edward Meryon actually described the disease before Duchenne did, but it was already named Duchenne MD when this was discovered.

DMD affects only boys and occurs in about one in 3,500 births. Most affected boys do not survive beyond their teens or early adulthood. Symptoms usually start between ages two and six, although in some cases they begin earlier. Logan, for example, was diagnosed with DMD at age sixteen months. As his mother explains:

> When Logan was a year old, he wasn't pulling himself up or couldn't sit up from the laying position on his own, so our family doctor referred us to a pediatrician. At that appointment, the pediatrician said to give him another couple of months. So, when he was 16 months and still not trying to walk or crawl, we took him back. They took his blood to "rule out" a muscle disorder. The next day they called to tell us he had DMD.[9]

In slightly older boys, first symptoms of DMD often include falling and difficulty running, walking, getting up stairs, and rising from a seated position. The child's calf muscles may look enlarged due to fat replacing muscle tissue. Soon, the boy will walk on his toes with the abdomen pushed forward because of pelvic muscle weakness. The shoulders may be pushed back and the child may not be able to raise his arms due to weakness of the shoulder muscles.

Scoliosis, or curvature of the spine, and tightness of the muscles known as contractures are common. Contractures can occur in the knees, hips, elbows, wrists, and fingers, making the joints painful and difficult to move. Many boys with DMD also have contracted Achilles tendons (heel cords that attach the muscles at the back of the lower legs to the heel bone) that result in feet that are angled abnormally. By age twelve, most boys with DMD cannot walk.

DMD also affects the heart and breathing muscles. Weakness of the heart muscle is known as cardiomyopathy and eventually can lead to heart failure. Weakness in the diaphragm (the muscle under the lungs that pulls in air and squeezes it out) and other muscles that control breathing often leads to breathing problems, which are in fact the leading cause of death from DMD. Weakness in the breathing muscles can also lead to an inability to cough. Patients who lose the ability to cough often get infections in the lungs.

Guillame Benjamin Amand Duchenne

Guillame Duchenne was born into a family of sea captains and fishermen in Boulogne, France, in 1806. He decided to enter the field of medicine despite his father's efforts to convince him to become a sailor. Duchenne graduated from medical school in Paris, and then returned to Boulogne to practice. He married in 1831, and when his wife died during childbirth, his mother-in-law spread rumors that Duchenne was responsible for her death. Duchenne became severely depressed and nearly abandoned his medical practice. A few years later, though, his interest in the new technique of using electrical coils to diagnose and treat diseases of the muscles and nerves led him to move to Paris to pursue research on this topic. His work on electrical stimulation established him as a pioneer in the field of neurology and resulted in numerous awards.

Starting in 1861 he wrote about several boys with the form of muscular dystrophy that now bears his name. He called the disease "paralysie musculaire pseudohypertrophique," which means muscular paralysis with enlarged muscles due to fatty deposits replacing muscle tissue. The name was later changed to Duchenne muscular dystrophy. Duchenne died in 1875 from a brain hemorrhage.

About one-third of boys with DMD have mental impairments resulting in difficulty reading, understanding words, and remembering things. Scientists believe these problems result from biological changes in the brain brought about by missing chemicals in people with the disease. This intellectual impairment generally does not get progressively worse like the muscle weakness does.

Becker Muscular Dystrophy

Another type of MD is Becker muscular dystrophy (BMD), named after Dr. Peter Emil Becker of the University of Göttingen in Germany, who first described the disorder in the mid 1950s. Like Duchenne muscular dystrophy, Becker MD affects males, but symptoms start later than those in DMD and are less severe. Becker MD usually becomes apparent in the teens or early twenties and occurs in about one in thirty thousand male births in the United States. Early symptoms include walking on the toes, waddling, frequent falls, and difficulty getting up from the floor. Muscles in the arms are also weakened. Calf muscles may appear large as fat replaces muscle. Despite the muscle weakness, many men with BMD live long, active lives. Some, however, die early because of cardiomyopathy and breathing problems associated with the disease.

Emery-Dreifuss Muscular Dystrophy

Emery-Dreifuss muscular dystrophy (EDMD) was first described in the mid 1960s by Fritz Dreifuss of Charlottesville, Virginia, and Alan E.H. Emery of Great Britain. EDMD is very rare, and only about three hundred cases have been identified in the United States. It mostly affects boys, though girls can sometimes get the disease. According to a Muscular Dystrophy Association publication on the rare muscular dystrophies, "Emery-Dreifuss muscular dystrophy is characterized by wasting and weakness of the muscles that make up the shoulders and upper arms and those of the calf muscles in the legs. Another prominent aspect of this disease is the appearance of contractures (stiff joints) in the elbows, neck and heels very early in the course of the disease. . . . The symptoms of EDMD usually become apparent by 10 years of age, but the disorder tends to progress slowly."[10]

Early symptoms of EDMD include tripping over carpets and steps, walking on the toes, inability to fully extend the elbows, and difficulty bending the neck forward. Later on when the pelvic muscles become weak the patient may not be able to walk. Since this form of MD tends to progress slowly, many affected by it survive into middle age. Some, however, die earlier from a serious condition called heart block. Heart block is also called a cardiac arrhythmia. An arrhythmia is an irregular heartbeat. The electrical pacing system that regulates the heartbeat can malfunction and result in a heart rate that is too fast or too slow, either of which can reduce the amount of blood pumped by the heart. Heart block occurs when the heart rate is too slow. This can lead to dizziness, fainting, fatigue, shortness of breath, and possibly heart failure.

Some patients also develop cardiomyopathy due to a weakened heart muscle. William Groh, a heart specialist at Indiana University, explains that the heart problems involved in EDMD can make the disease very serious: "In the past, people have defined Emery-Dreifuss as a not very severe form of muscular dystrophy, because the skeletal muscle involvement hasn't been as severe, but that's not been true about the heart involvement."[11]

Limb-Girdle Muscular Dystrophy

Limb-girdle muscular dystrophy (LGMD) is rare in North America but more common in Brazil and northern Africa for unknown reasons. It affects both males and females, primarily weakening muscles around the hips and shoulders—the so-called pelvic and shoulder girdles, or limb girdles. Weakness is usually first noticed in the hip area, followed by the shoulders, legs, and neck. Patients tend to waddle and have difficulty rising from a chair or climbing stairs. Many fall frequently and are unable to run. Contractures in the back muscles are common, giving the appearance of a rigid spine. Some patients experience heart and breathing problems that can lead to death. Heart problems can take the form of cardiomyopathy or cardiac arrhythmias. The brain, senses, and digestive system are not affected in LGMD.

Doctors have identified fourteen different subtypes of LGMD that differ in age of onset and severity. Some forms begin in childhood or adolescence and are usually more severe than forms that begin in adulthood. However, there is a great deal of variability in progression and severity within the subtypes of LGMD, as the Muscular Dystrophy Association points out, "Some forms of the disorder progress to loss of walking ability within a few years, while others progress very slowly over many years and cause minimal disability. At this time, progression in each type of LGMD can't be predicted with certainty."[12]

Curvature of the spine caused by weakened abdominal muscles is one of many effects of facioscapulohumeral muscular dystrophy (FSHMD)

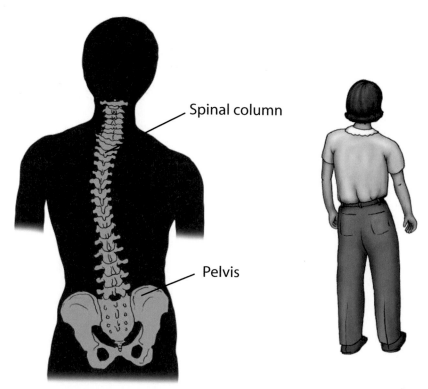

Spinal column

Pelvis

Facioscapulohumeral Muscular Dystrophy

Facioscapulohumeral muscular dystrophy (FSHMD or FSHD), also known as Landouzy-Dejerine disease, usually begins in adolescence or early adulthood. Rarely, it affects young children, and when this happens the disease is usually more severe than in adolescents or adults. FSHMD primarily affects muscles in the face (facio), shoulders (scapulo), and upper arms (humera). The shoulders slope forward. The person has difficulty raising his or her arms over the head. The eyes cannot close properly; when this happens during sleep, the person may awaken with dry, burning eyes that are prone to serious injury from the dryness. Hearing loss is frequent. Patients may not be able to whistle or drink through a straw. The lips may appear to pout, and speech may be garbled. Unlike other types of muscular dystrophy, FSHMD can affect muscles on one side of the body more than the other side at the beginning of the disease.

As FSHMD progresses, muscle weakness can spread to other areas of the body, particularly the pelvis, lower legs, and feet, resulting in tripping, falling, and difficulty walking. Muscles in the abdomen may also be affected, leading to a curved spine because abdominal weakness puts pressure on the spine. As the author of *Muscular Dystrophy: The Facts* explains, the progression of FSHMD varies widely:

> More than any other type of dystrophy, the expression of this disease varies considerably from one person to another, sometimes within the same family. Some may have only mild facial weakness and no more than minimal shoulder weakness all their lives which may even go unrecognized. About half never have any pelvic girdle weakness which causes them serious problems. However some, fortunately few, eventually become confined to a wheelchair. Life expectancy in general is not significantly reduced and many remain active throughout their lives. The heart is not affected and there is no intellectual impairment.[13]

Distal Muscular Dystrophy

Distal muscular dystrophy (DD), also known as distal myopathy, usually begins in adulthood and can affect men and women. It begins with weakness in the muscles most distant from the center of the body, such as the forearms, hands, lower legs, and feet. Weakness may progress to include other muscles in the body like the upper legs, neck, heart, and breathing muscles, although the number of muscles affected by DD tends to be less than in other forms of muscular dystrophy. Early signs of DD are clumsiness when buttoning clothing, typing, or dialing a phone. Tripping over carpets and steps is common. The affected person cannot stand on his or her heels and sometimes cannot stand on the toes.

Distal muscular dystrophy has several subtypes. One subtype is Welander's distal myopathy. Onset of this disorder tends to occur in people between forty and fifty years of age and first affects the arms and hands, then the legs. Another subtype is Finnish, or tibial, muscular dystrophy. This usually begins after age forty and first affects muscles over the tibia bone in the lower legs. It progresses slowly to involve the arms, hands, trunk muscles, and sometimes the heart. Finnish distal myopathy affects only people of Finnish descent. In Myoshi distal myopathy, weakness begins in the calf muscles and progresses to other muscles. Myoshi DD begins between ages fifteen and thirty. There are several other subtypes of DD that begin at a variety of ages and which involve different muscle groups.

Oculopharyngeal Muscular Dystrophy

Oculopharyngeal muscular dystrophy (OPMD) affects men and women and begins in a person's thirties, forties, or fifties. In the United States and Canada the disease most often affects families of French Canadian descent and Hispanics in northern New Mexico. OPMD is characterized by weakness in the muscles that control the eyelids (oculo means eye) and pharyngeal muscles (muscles in the throat that control swallowing and speech). The first symptom is drooping eyelids, uncoordinated eye movements, and double vision, followed by facial weakness and difficulty swallowing. The swallowing problems can lead to nutritional deficiencies and to inhaling food or liquids into the lungs, which can result in pneumonia. Sometimes OPMD affects the voice, and the tongue may shrink. Some patients may also develop weakness in the neck, shoulders, and limbs, leading to difficulties in reaching, walking, kneeling, or bending.

Congenital Muscular Dystrophy

Types of MD that appear in newborn babies or within a few months of birth are collectively referred to as congenital muscular dystrophy (CMD). These diseases may not be diagnosed right away, but most babies who have them show immediate signs of muscle weakness and poor muscle tone. The Muscular Dystrophy Association says that "a diagnosis of CMD can be confusing because for many years the term was used as a 'catchall' name to describe conditions that looked like other muscular dystrophies, but started much earlier . . . in recent years doctors have agreed that there are several different categories of 'true' CMD, and they're distinct from other muscular dystrophies."[14]

CMD can affect both boys and girls. Some subtypes are severe, such as when a baby is "floppy" at birth with no muscle tone. Such babies rarely learn to walk and often have reduced intelligence. They have breathing problems that may be fatal and usually die in infancy or early childhood. Other forms of CMD are not as severe and the child may learn to walk and live into his or her twenties.

One subtype of CMD is merosin deficient CMD. Children with this form lack a protein called merosin in their muscles. Some of these children are eventually able to walk, while others are not. Some have muscle contractures, breathing problems, and seizures. Intelligence is usually normal. This form of CMD progresses slowly. Another subtype of CMD, integrin deficient CMD, also involves lack of a protein and includes poor muscle tone and the inability to walk until age two or three.

Ullrich CMD includes loss of muscle tone, loose joints in the hands and feet, rigidity of the spine, and joint contractures at birth. Breathing difficulties are common, though intelligence is normal.

Fukuyama CMD, named for Yukio Fukuyama of Tokyo, Japan, who first described it in 1960, is rarely seen outside of Japan. Many affected children are able to crawl, but few ever walk. Many have enlarged calves, are severely mentally retarded, and have epilepsy, a disease that results in brain seizures. Death in childhood is common, though some patients live into their twenties.

Walker-Warburg syndrome is similar to Fukuyama CMD, but it is much more severe. Characterized by lack of muscle tone, severe mental retardation, and vision problems, Walker–Warburg syndrome is usually fatal during infancy.

Cataracts, or the clouding of the interior lens of the eye, can develop in people with myotonic muscular dystrophy, which affects the muscles in many areas of the body.

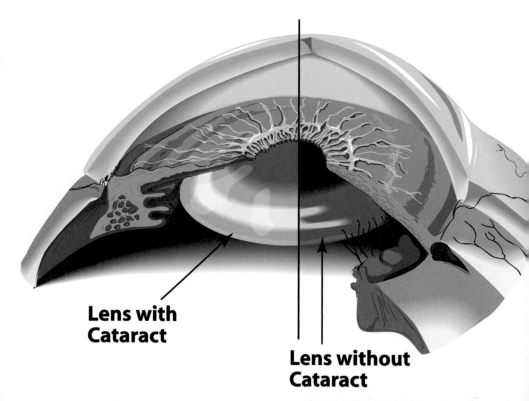

Lens with Cataract

Lens without Cataract

Myotonic Muscular Dystrophy

In myotonic muscular dystrophy (MMD), also known as Steinert's disease, the primary feature is that the muscles cannot relax. Myotonia is prolonged stiffening of and inability to relax the muscles. Many people with MMD have difficulty letting go of things they are holding and often involuntarily clench their hands or jaw. After sneezing the individual may not be able to relax the muscles around the eyes. Smooth and heart muscles may also not be able to relax, and this can lead to problems with the heartbeat, food getting stuck in the esophagus, intestinal cramps, and difficulties for women during childbirth.

MMD also involves muscle weakness in many areas of the body. This generally first appears in the face, neck, feet, and hands. Weakness in muscles that pick up the feet often leads to the feet flopping downward, resulting in tripping and falling. Weakness in facial muscles may give the face an appearance of being long and thin, and the eyelids often droop. Weakness in involuntary muscles in the heart, lungs, central nervous system, and digestive tract can lead to difficulties in breathing, swallowing, speaking, and hearing. Some people with MMD develop a mild type of diabetes known as insulin resistance. Here, the pancreas produces insulin, which is needed to metabolize sugars, but the body does not let the insulin do its job, so the sugar builds up in the bloodstream. Many people with MMD also develop cataracts, or cloudy lenses in the eyes. Cataracts are not related to muscle weakness, and it is unknown why they occur frequently in patients with MMD.

Most cases of MMD begin in the twenties and thirties, but some with severe cases show symptoms at birth. Generally, the earlier it begins, the more severe is the disease. Doctors have identified two subtypes of MMD: type 1 MMD, or MMD1, and type 2 MMD or MMD2. MMD1 is more severe than MMD2.

CHAPTER TWO

Diagnosis and Treatment

Diagnosis of any type of muscular dystrophy can be difficult because the various forms sometimes resemble each other or look like other muscle diseases. If a primary care physician suspects that a patient may have MD, he or she will refer the person to a neurologist, who is a specialist in nerve and muscle diseases, or to a pediatrician, who specializes in disorders affecting children. As the disease progresses, other specialists may be called in to diagnose and treat problems like heart weakness or breathing difficulties.

A doctor diagnoses MD by first taking a medical history about symptoms, past health, and diseases that run in the family. Then he or she performs a physical examination and does certain tests that measure how well the patient's nerves and muscles work.

Some tests observe behavior, such as watching how easily the patient rises from the floor and from a seated position, hops on the toes, walks on the heels, and raises the arms overhead. The doctor also checks reflexes and muscle strength by using a reflex hammer and having the patient perform certain exercises.

Laboratory Tests

Laboratory tests also help doctors diagnose MD. One important laboratory test is an electromyograph, or EMG. This meas-

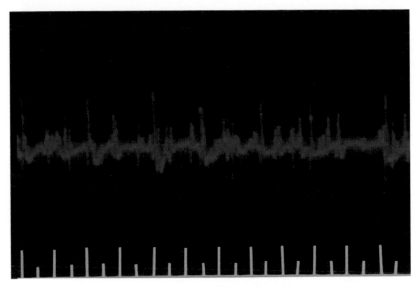

The wave pattern generated by an electromyograph (EMG) tells doctors how much electrical activity is produced by a muscle when it contracts. An EMG is one of several laboratory tests that help determine if a person has muscular dystrophy.

ures electrical activity in a muscle. Muscles produce electrical activity when they contract. The doctor inserts a needle called an electrode into a muscle and asks the patient to move that muscle. The electrode is hooked up to a machine called an oscilloscope, which displays the muscle's electrical activity in the form of a wave. These waves are called action potentials, and their size and shape tell the doctor how well the muscle is functioning. People with MD generally have abnormally small action potentials. The EMG cannot, however, be used to distinguish the different types of MD. It is also difficult to use with small children, since it is very painful and requires the patient to cooperate and contract a particular muscle, so other diagnostic tests are used as well.

Doctors often perform a muscle biopsy, where they remove a small piece of muscle tissue with a needle or by cutting it out. This is done with local anesthesia that numbs the area. The doctor then looks at the muscle tissue under a microscope. People with MD typically show very large or very small muscle fibers (single muscle cells that comprise muscle tissue) that are dead or dying. The physician can also stain the muscle fibers with certain chemical dyes to reveal protein and gene abnormalities present in different types of muscular dystrophy.

Doctors also do nerve conduction studies to measure how fast electrical signals travel along a nerve. A small electrode placed in one spot along the nerve sends a signal to a receiving electrode placed elsewhere along the nerve, and the time it takes for the signal to travel is measured. This test can help a physician figure out whether the person is suffering from a muscle disorder like MD or from a problem with the nerves that control the muscles.

To determine the presence and degree of heart damage, a physician will often order an electrocardiogram (EKG). An EKG translates the heart's electrical activity into line tracings on paper using an EKG machine. It can be used to diagnose abnormal heart rhythms and sometimes can detect cardiomyopathy. Another test called an echocardiogram, which uses ultrasound waves to obtain images of the inside of the heart, is better suited for diagnosing cardiomyopathy and is thus often used for this purpose.

Blood Tests

Besides these tests, doctors also order blood tests that check for certain enzymes. Enzymes are proteins that cause chemical changes in the body. The primary blood test that is useful in diagnosing MD is a test for the enzyme creatine kinase. This enzyme helps transform the chemical creatine into phosphocreatine, which is burned as a source of energy for all cells, including muscle cells. Many people with MD have abnormally high levels of creatine kinase in their blood because the enzyme leaks out of diseased muscles and into the bloodstream. The level seen in patients with Duchenne MD, in particular, can be fifty to one hundred times the normal level. Patients with other forms of MD such as limb-girdle, Emery-Dreifuss, and facioscapulohumeral have moderately elevated creatine kinase in their blood, up to ten times the normal level.

Diagnosing Muscular Dystrophy

Although a measurement of creatine kinase is the most widely used blood test in diagnosing muscular dystrophy, there are other assessments that can be useful. One is a test for blood levels of aldolase, an enzyme involved in the breakdown of glucose and other sugars used to provide energy to cells. Aldolase is particularly concentrated in muscle cells, and a high level of this enzyme in the blood is an indication that damaged muscle cells are leaking it into the bloodstream. High levels of the protein myoglobin in the urine can also indicate MD. Myoglobin is present in heart and skeletal muscles. When muscles are damaged, myoglobin can be released into the bloodstream, filtered out of the bloodstream by the kidneys, and excreted in the urine. Sometimes physicians will also measure the level of lactic acid dehydrogenase, an enzyme that is released into the blood when muscle or other tissue damage is present. However, a high reading of lactic acid dehydrogenase may indicate the presence of diseases other than MD, such as liver disease, cancer, and certain blood diseases, so it is not a definitive method of testing for muscular dystrophy.

Imaging Tests

Imaging tests like ultrasound, computerized tomography (CT), and magnetic resonance imaging (MRI) can be used in diagnosing whether or not a patient has MD, but not in differentiating the forms. These tests can detect significant changes in diseased muscles. Ultrasound tests use high frequency sound waves to obtain images inside the body. CT scans use special X-ray equipment to produce pictures of a patient's insides, and a computer joins these pictures together in cross-sectional views and displays them on a screen. MRI machines create a magnetic field around the body. Radio waves are then passed through the body to trigger a signal that is processed by a computer into a two or three dimensional picture.

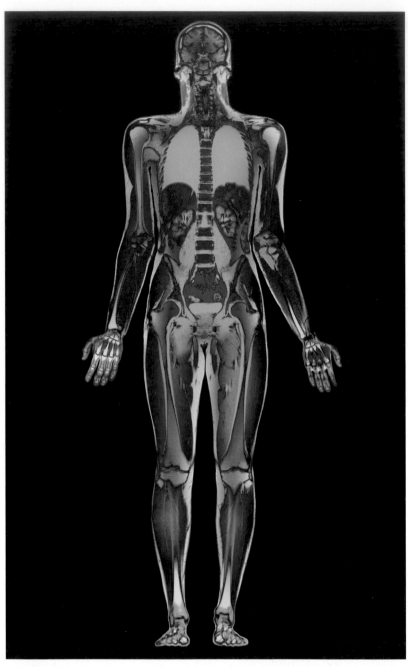

Magnetic resonance imaging (MRI) scans like the one here are among the imaging tests used to diagnose muscular dystrophy.

Treatment Plans

Once a doctor has diagnosed a patient with MD, he or she will tailor a treatment plan to the individual's needs. According to the National Institute of Neurological Disorders and Stroke:

> There is no specific treatment that can stop or reverse the progress of any form of MD . . . Treatment is aimed at keeping the patient independent for as long as possible and preventing complications that result from weakness, reduced mobility, and cardiac and respiratory difficulties. Treatment may involve a combination of approaches, including physical therapy, drug therapy, and surgery.[15]

All treatment plans include a physician encouraging the patient to maintain general good health by eating a well-balanced diet that includes plenty of fresh fruits and vegetables. This helps prevent too much weight gain from immobility and also reduces constipation, which is a common problem in people with MD. Doctors also encourage the patient to do moderately active exercise for as long as possible without becoming exhausted.

Physical Therapy

Often a physician will send a patient to a physical therapist who specializes in designing appropriate exercise programs for people with disabilities. Swimming is one activity that physical therapists prescribe for MD patients because it does not place much strain on the muscles. Even those who are usually in a wheelchair can sometimes get out of the chair and into a swimming pool with help. Parent Project Muscular Dystrophy (PPMD), an organization that provides support to people with Duchenne and Becker MD, says swimming is good for several reasons: "Most young men enjoy swimming or hydrotherapy [water therapy], which is a wonderful way of stretching out and moving freely without too much effort. It also provides good respiratory exercise but most of all it will allow him to have some fun with family and friends out of his chair."[16]

Hydrotherapy sessions are frequently prescribed for people with muscular dystrophy because the water buoys the muscles, allowing them to stretch and move freely.

When certain exercises or movements become impossible for patients to perform on their own, physical therapists recommend passive exercise. This refers to the movement of the patient's limbs by another person and is designed to maintain mobility and prevent muscle contractures. Passive exercise can be done by a physical therapist or by family members who have been taught to correctly perform it. It includes gentle stretching and must be done regularly for the most benefit. Once muscle contractures occur, passive exercise does not help and may actually harm the muscles and joints, so starting therapy before contractures start is important.

Occupational Therapy

Physical therapists sometimes recommend and help the patient obtain assistive equipment like wheelchairs, but more often this is done by an occupational therapist. Occupational therapists assess the need for special equipment or modifications to the home that enable a patient to perform basic activities like getting around, eating, and dressing. "Anything which makes an individual's life more independent and enables the continued pursuit of employment, or even interesting pastimes and hobbies, has to be encouraged," says the author of *Muscular Dystrophy: The Facts.*[17]

Assistance for the disabled can include special devices such as easy-grab tableware or Velcro fasteners on clothing and shoes. Computer companies now make computers that can be adapted for people with weak muscles. Patients whose eyelids droop significantly can be helped by special glasses that are equipped with "eyelid crutches" to hold the eyes open. Those who cannot close the eyes completely, as often happens in FSHMD, may have to use eye shields at night to keep their eyes from drying out while they sleep. Many people with MD benefit from elevated toilet seats, bathroom grab bars, easy lift chairs that help them rise from a seated position, ramps and wheelchair accessible showers installed in the home, special mattresses that relieve pressure on the body, and walkers or leg braces to help with standing or walking. The Muscular Dystrophy Association points out that standing up is important for

Computers with special keyboards to accommodate the needs of people with disabilities are among the many daily tools that are available for use by people with muscular dystrophy.

patients who are able to do so: "Standing for a few hours each day, even with minimal weight bearing, promotes better circulation, healthier bones and a straight spine."[18]

Many boys with Duchenne MD have abnormally angled feet due to contractures in the Achilles tendons of the ankles and must wear ankle-straightening splints to help keep their feet straight. Patients with many types of MD develop scoliosis, the curving of the spine to one side. They can slow this process by using custom-made back supports, braces, or plastic splints that extend from the buttocks to the ankles.

Those patients who need a wheelchair must be carefully fitted for one that is comfortable and provides adequate back support. It cannot be too wide or too narrow, must have proper support for the head if needed, and must be the correct height from the floor. Some wheelchairs have special arm supports and lap boards to help the patient work while seated. Others have adjustable foot rests or foot wedges that keep the ankles slightly bent to avoid muscle contractures, and some have extended leg rests to prevent contractures in the knees. Both manual and power wheelchairs are available, depending on the needs of the patient.

Speech and Swallowing Therapy

Patients with weakened facial or throat muscles may require speech therapy so they can continue to communicate by voice. Speech therapists assist the person with learning to articulate words despite weakened muscles. If speech becomes impossible, a speech therapist can recommend computer experts who will put together a special computer with a voice synthesizer that is used for communication.

A speech therapist is also trained to assist patients who have trouble chewing and swallowing. Oftentimes the speech therapist will work with a nutritionist to develop a plan that insures the patient receives adequate nutrition. At first, eating pureed foods and drinking thick liquids such as milkshakes, which are easier to swallow than thin liquids, may be sufficient. Holding the head in different positions can also help swallowing. Sometimes, though, a patient's weak swallowing muscles cause food to be sucked into the lungs instead of into the esophagus. This can lead to pneumonia. If this or choking on food happens, the patient may need to be fed with a feeding tube. Here, a doctor who specializes in the gastrointestinal system inserts a plastic tube through a hole in the abdomen into the stomach. Liquid nutrients are then pumped through the tube into the stomach.

Breathing Therapy

Breathing problems from weakness in the respiratory muscles often lead to death in MD patients, so doctors perform frequent lung function tests to make sure infections or lung failure are not developing. Physicians who specialize in assessing and treating breathing problems are called pulmonologists.

Pulmonologists often recommend deep breathing exercises for those who experience mild breathing difficulties. Patients whose muscles become so weak that they cannot cough are often affected by mucous accumulating in the lungs. This can

A therapist performs postural drainage techniques on a patient in order to loosen mucus in the lungs that can build up when muscle weakness inhibits the ability to cough.

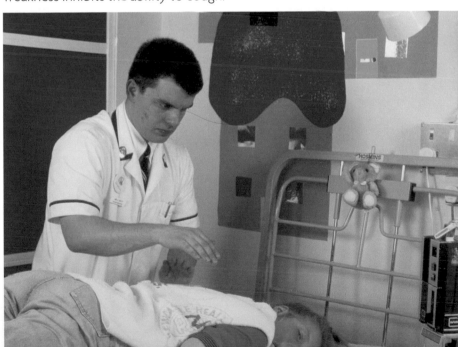

be treated with a drainage technique in which the person lies face down with the head lower than the chest. A respiratory therapist or trained family member clasps the lower part of the chest with a cupped hand at the same time as the patient is instructed to try to cough. The mucous that comes up into the throat is then removed. As an alternative, some patients use a coughing machine. This machine includes a mask that shoots a blast of air into the lungs to help the person cough.

For those with severe breathing difficulties, assisted ventilation may be necessary. Serious breathing problems usually become apparent first during sleep, so, at least initially, assisted

Treating Cardiomyopathy in Muscular Dystrophy Patients

Doctors often prescribe ACE inhibitors or beta blockers for MD patients affected by cardiomyopathy. ACE inhibitors work by slowing the activity of angiotensin converting enzyme, a protein in the body that combines with a chemical called angiotensin 2. Angiotensin 2 then causes the muscles around blood vessels to contract, thereby narrowing the blood vessels. This can result in high blood pressure that makes it harder for the heart to pump. ACE inhibitors reduce blood pressure and thus make it easier for the heart to do its work. Beta blockers are drugs that block adrenaline and other chemicals in the body that lead to high blood pressure, fast heart rate, and blood vessel contractions. These drugs are often used to reduce stress on the heart by slowing the heart rate and lessening the force of each heart muscle contraction.

Researchers have found that treatment with ACE inhibitors or beta blockers can slow heart muscle damage in MD patients if the medication is started when abnormalities on an echocardiogram (ultrasound image of the heart) are detected. These abnormalities usually become apparent before any symptoms of heart failure begin.

ventilation may be required only at night. Most patients use an intermittent positive pressure ventilator for this purpose. This is a machine connected to a tube that goes into the nose or mouth or into a mask that covers the face. The machine pushes an ongoing amount of air into the lungs.

When lung function deteriorates to the point of failing day and night, the patient may need what is called invasive ventilation, or a tracheostomy. Here, a doctor inserts a tube into a hole that is cut in the windpipe. The tube is connected to a ventilator that pumps air into the lungs.

Surgeries for Muscular Dystrophy

Other complications of MD require various types of surgery as treatment. One frequently performed surgery releases the muscles in a joint locked by contractures. This is often done on the heel cords when the patient is experiencing ankle contractures and is still capable of walking. This type of surgery, however, can further weaken muscles, so it must be used sparingly. Most people who undergo heel cord surgery must wear foot or leg braces afterwards.

Patients whose eyelids are affected by MD can have surgery to prop up the drooping eyelids. Those with cataracts, or cloudy eye lenses that can restrict vision, often receive cataract surgery, where the doctor removes the lenses and installs artificial ones.

In FSHMD and some other forms of the disease, weakened shoulder muscles prevent the person from raising the arms, and this can be corrected by a surgical procedure that fastens the shoulder blade to the ribs. The shoulder blade then does not slide around and this makes it easier for the person to move the arm.

Scoliosis is often a serious problem because it can result in compression of one lung as well as in discomfort. Surgery that straightens the spine and wires the individual vertebrae to stainless steel rods fixed to the spine can correct scoliosis and prevent future curving of the spine. Another type of operation called a spinal fusion can also be used for this purpose. Here, the surgeon inserts pieces of bone in between the vertebrae to fuse them together, thus straightening the spine. Either type of surgery can help preserve lung function and make sitting more comfortable.

Patients with heart problems related to MD can benefit from several types of procedures. Those with a heart arrhythmia that results in a heart rate that is too fast or too slow may need to have a pacemaker implanted in their chest by a surgeon. Pacemakers are machines about the size of a small mp3 player. Wires attached to the pacemaker are connected to the heart and measure the heart's activity. When the pacemaker receives data that indicate the heart rate is too slow or too fast, it delivers impulses that correct the heart rate. A doctor can repro-

An X-ray shows the placement of a pacemaker inside a patient's chest. A person who develops heart problems as a result of muscular dystrophy may be given a pacemaker in order to regulate heart rate.

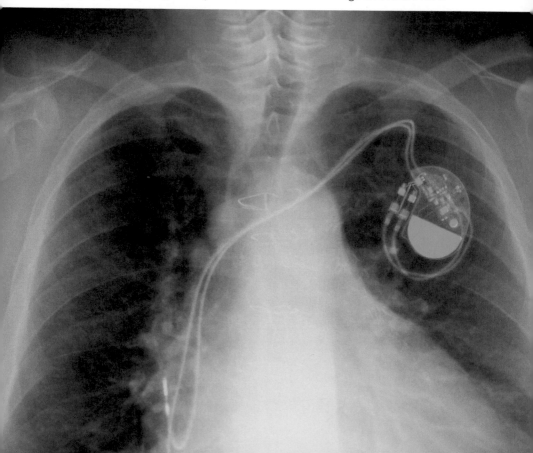

gram the pacemaker if the patient's needs change. Sometimes a surgeon will implant a cardioverter-defibrillator along with a pacemaker. This device delivers an electric shock to reset the heartbeat if heart failure occurs.

Another method of regulating heart arrhythmias is surgery to remove damaged cells that regulate the heartbeat. A surgeon inserts a thin tube through a large blood vessel into the heart and destroys groups of abnormal cells by burning, freezing, or using radio waves. The doctor is guided to the correct area of the heart by imaging machines that display the inside of the heart on a computer screen.

When heart problems become so severe that they are not helped by a pacemaker or by medication, some patients receive a heart transplant. In this procedure, surgeons place the heart of a donor into the patient whose own heart is failing. This type of operation is generally done on patients who are otherwise fairly healthy, such as men with Becker MD who have minimal disability due to voluntary muscle weakness. Even relatively healthy people who receive a transplant are severely weakened by the surgery, though, and the recipient's body can reject the donor heart even when he or she is given antirejection drugs.

Drug Treatments

Before a doctor sends an MD patient for surgery, he or she will generally try prescribing medicines to alleviate various complications of the disease for which drug treatments exist. Unfortunately, many of the problems that go along with MD do not respond well to medications, at least for long-term treatment. For example, muscle relaxing drugs such as diphenylhydantoin, mexiletine, and baclofen can give short-term relief from the prolonged muscle stiffness seen in myotonic muscular dystrophy, but fail to make the problem go away for very long. A great many drugs have also been tried in an attempt to slow muscle degeneration in people with all types of MD, but none succeeds in the long run.

Prednisone, a synthetic form of the steroid hormone cortisone (which is naturally produced by the adrenal glands under the kidneys), has been used for over twenty years to slow muscle degeneration, but it has severe side effects and does not delay this degeneration for more than a couple of years. Recent research shows that prednisone allows boys with Duchenne MD to continue walking for up to two years longer than they would have without the drug. However, these boys also experience frequent bone fractures as a side effect of prednisone, which causes thinning of the bones. Other serious side effects include weight gain, high blood pressure, high blood sugar, acne, and suppression of the immune system with a subsequent inability to fight infections. Doctors are now trying to reduce side effects by using prednisone only on alternate days or by prescribing a related steroid that has fewer side effects, but so far this has not led to improvements in the patients' condition. Experts disagree as to when steroids should be started, as explained by the Muscular Dystrophy Association:

> The optimal age to begin treatment with corticosteroids has not been determined. Some physicians believe corticosteroids should be started as soon as the diagnosis is made, while others prefer to wait until a boy is having difficulty walking. Before starting treatment with corticosteroids, the physician and the family should have a balanced discussion about anticipated benefits and potential side effects.[19]

The heart disorders that often accompany MD can be treated with several drugs that help preserve heart function. Patients with cardiomyopathy can benefit from angiotensin converting enzyme (ACE) inhibitors and beta blockers that reduce the strain on the heart muscle. Patients with heart arrhythmias can sometimes be helped by drugs which change the flow of chemicals that influence the heartbeat. These medications include amiodarone, digoxin, and quinidine. When these drugs do not work, the patient usually receives a pacemaker.

CHAPTER THREE

What Causes Muscular Dystrophy?

All forms of muscular dystrophy are caused by degeneration in the muscles. Muscles are made of thousands of muscle fibers bound together by connective tissue. The muscle fibers are activated when the brain sends a signal along the nerves that connect the brain and spinal cord to other parts of the body. Chemicals called neurotransmitters relay signals from the brain to the muscle fibers and they contract or relax in response.

When a person has muscular dystrophy, the membrane surrounding the muscle fibers or other parts of the muscle cells are damaged, and the muscle fibers begin to leak creatine kinase and to take on excess calcium. This further damages the cells, and soon the muscle fibers die. The damaged or dead muscle cells can no longer respond to signals from the brain telling them to move. This causes the muscle weakness seen in all types of MD, and this weakness and subsequent inactivity leads to other symptoms like contractures. A gene mutation is the root cause of the muscle damage and disability.

Genes and Muscular Dystrophy

Genes are the part of DNA that transmit hereditary information from parents to their offspring. People have about thirty thousand genes that are located on worm-shaped bodies called chromosomes in the nucleus, or center, of each cell. The sequence of genes on each chromosome provides the cell with a set of

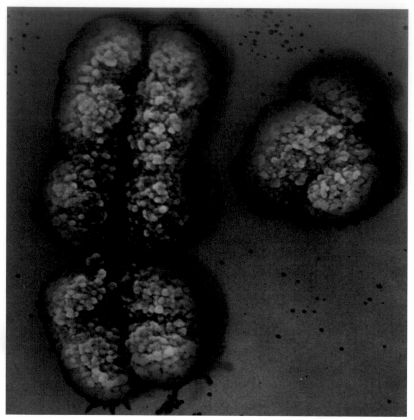

Human chromosomes contain genetic material that, if mutated, can result in a person having certain diseases, including muscular dystrophy.

instructions on how to grow and operate. A baby is born with two copies of instructions—one from each parent.

Every cell in the human body has forty-six chromosomes. Twenty-three come from the mother and twenty-three from the father, and together they form twenty-three pairs. Twenty-two of the pairs of chromosomes are called autosomes. The remaining pair are known as sex chromosomes because they determine whether a person is male or female. Females have two X sex chromosomes, and males have an X and a Y chromosome. The genes on each chromosome also come in pairs. In each pair, one gene comes from the mother and one from the father.

When a gene or chromosome is damaged, this results in a change called a mutation. Mutated genetic material can be passed from either the mother or father to a child. This can lead to various malfunctions and produce certain diseases. Sometimes mutations result from damage to the genes or chromosomes that occurs after a child is born, but this is not the case in muscular dystrophy. With MD, "In some families the mutant gene which causes the disease can be traced back several generations. In others, the causative mutation occurs in the egg or sperm which led to that particular affected individual,"[20] says the author of *Muscular Dystrophy: The Facts*.

Since a child inherits one gene in each gene pair from the mother and one from the father, this child can inherit either two normal genes, two abnormal genes, or one normal and one abnormal gene. When the child inherits two normal or two abnormal genes, he or she is said to be homozygous for that trait. When the two genes are different, the individual is heterozygous. The mutant gene, furthermore, can be recessive or dominant. When it is recessive in a heterozygote, it is suppressed or overpowered by the normal gene in the pair, so it is not expressed and the person does not get the associated illness. However, a person with one recessive mutant gene becomes a carrier of the mutation and can pass it on when he or she reproduces. A person with two recessive genes will get the illness caused by the mutation. If a mutant gene is dominant it is expressed in a heterozygote and the person gets the disease. Thus, in order for an individual to be affected by a particular genetic disease, either two recessive mutant genes or one dominant mutant gene must be present, except in the case of X-linked recessive traits such as Duchenne or Becker muscular dystrophy, where a male who has only one copy of the mutant recessive gene can get the disease.

Causes of Genetic Diseases

Genetic diseases are caused by mutant genes on either the X chromosome or on one of the twenty-two pairs of autosomes. There are no known diseases that are caused by mutations

Genetic Testing and Privacy Concerns

Since scientists have now identified many of the gene mutations that cause various types of muscular dystrophy, this information can be valuable in diagnosing a particular form of MD, identifying disease carriers, or predicting the future occurrence of MD in a family member. Using genetic testing to aid in diagnosing diseases or in determining whether an individual is a carrier so he or she can decide whether or not to have children is generally not controversial. However, performing these tests on people who do not show any symptoms in order to assess their likelihood of later developing a disease has raised some privacy concerns. As the Muscular Dystrophy Association explains: "Some people are very concerned that genetic testing can interfere with privacy, insurance eligibility or even employment . . . laws protecting people who have had genetic testing from discrimination for insurance or employment are unclear and vary from state to state. Even general privacy rights can't be strictly guaranteed."

Muscular Dystrophy Association, "Genetics and Neuromuscular Diseases," April 2000. www.mda.org/publications/gen_test.html.

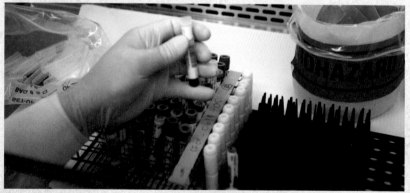

Samples of genetic material are subject to testing at a diagnostic laboratory. Advocates for privacy rights are concerned that genetic testing to diagnose or determine if a person carries a gene mutation tied to muscular dystrophy or other diseases can result in discrimination.

on the Y chromosome. Since genes can be either dominant or recessive, genetic diseases can be inherited in four possible ways: autosomal dominant, autosomal recessive, X-linked dominant, or X-linked recessive.

Thus far, the types of muscular dystrophy that doctors have identified are either autosomal dominant, autosomal recessive, or X-linked recessive. Those who inherit an autosomal dominant type of MD can be male or female, and the mutation can be passed on by one parent who has autosomal dominant MD. With autosomal recessive types of MD, a male or female child must inherit two mutated genes in order to develop the disease. This can happen if the child has two normal parents who are both carriers of an autosomal recessive mutation for MD or if he or she has one parent with MD and the other parent who is a carrier. In instances where two normal parents are carriers who pass on the disease, they will probably not know that they are carriers until they have a child who gets MD, unless they previously underwent genetic testing that revealed the gene abnormalities.

Only males can inherit forms of MD that are X-linked recessive. This is because females have two X chromosomes, and a mutation on one of the X chromosomes will be dominated by the normal gene on her other X chromosome. Theoretically, a girl could inherit a recessive X mutation from a father who has MD and a mother who is a carrier, but geneticists say this is very unlikely to happen. A boy who inherits an X chromosome with the mutant gene will get the associated disease since he does not have a second X chromosome to counter the effects.

Genes and Proteins

However they are inherited, the gene mutations that cause MD have incorrect or missing information that prevents them from making the proteins needed for healthy muscles. Proteins are chemical compounds made of building blocks called amino acids. They are responsible for building various structures in cells and for carrying out the functions of the cells. According

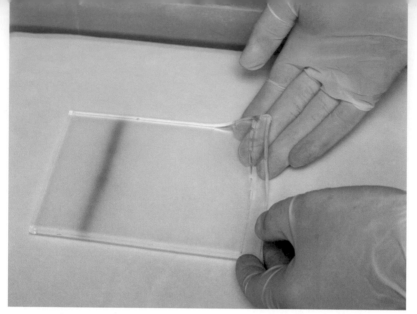

A researcher conducts a genetic test known as the Southern blot, in which an electrical current is used to separate DNA samples into fragments that reveal the presence of mutated genes.

to the Muscular Dystrophy Association genes issue instructions for manufacturing certain proteins in the following manner:

> The final copies of the protein recipes are actually carried in RNA (ribonucleic acid), a very close chemical cousin of DNA. The cell converts DNA to RNA in its nucleus. Each RNA recipe then leaves the cell's nucleus and becomes the instruction manual for the manufacturing of a protein outside the nucleus. A mutation in the DNA for any protein can become a mutation (error) in the RNA recipe and then an error in the protein made from those RNA instructions. Some mutations lead to production of a slightly abnormal protein, while others lead to a very abnormal protein or to the complete absence of a particular protein.[21]

Mutations in different genes that produce certain proteins cause the various forms of MD. Doctors can identify these gene mutations by performing molecular genetic tests on blood samples or muscle cells from a patient. One commonly employed test is the Southern blot, named after Edwin Southern, the scientist who invented it. Scientists perform a Southern blot by placing a DNA sample on a special gel and separating the DNA by applying an electrical current. The resulting DNA fragments are "blotted" onto a filter and identified using radioactive labels. This reveals whether or not a specific mutated gene is present. Another widely used genetic test is called polymerase chain reaction. This involves separating and replicating DNA using temperature changes and a chemical called a polymerase. Each DNA piece is then analyzed to locate gene mutations.

Duchenne Muscular Dystrophy

Duchenne MD is caused by mutations in the gene that makes the protein dystrophin. Dystrophin helps muscle cells keep their strength and shape, and lack of it weakens muscles. In DMD, the faulty gene does not produce any dystrophin. The faulty gene that causes DMD is an X-linked recessive gene,

A diagram of the inheritance pattern of Duchenne muscular dystrophy shows that sons have a 50-50 chance of inheriting the disorder from their mother if she carries the gene for it on one of her X chromosomes.

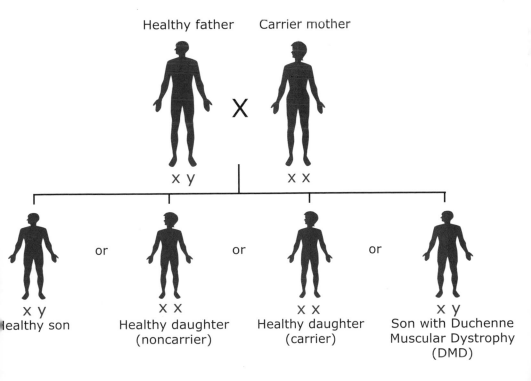

Healthy father   Carrier mother

X

x y   x x

or   or   or

x y   x x   x x   x y
Healthy son   Healthy daughter   Healthy daughter   Son with Duchenne
              (noncarrier)   (carrier)   Muscular Dystrophy
                                                    (DMD)

which is why only boys get DMD. Since boys with DMD generally do not survive long enough to have children, the disease is transmitted by women who are carriers of the abnormal gene. Sometimes, though, the mutation occurs in the egg of a woman who is not a carrier and is then expressed in a male child.

Becker Muscular Dystrophy

The mutated gene responsible for Becker MD is the same as that in Duchenne MD, but with Becker MD the gene does synthesize some dystrophin. The dystrophin is, however, abnormal or there is not enough of it. But, according to the Muscular Dystrophy Association, since people with BMD do have some dystrophin, "Having some dystrophin protects the muscles of those with Becker from degenerating as badly or as quickly as those of people with Duchenne."[22] This is why symptoms of BMD are less severe than in DMD.

Becker MD is an X-linked recessive disorder like DMD, so it rarely affects girls. But unlike DMD, where affected boys do not survive long enough to have children of their own, many men with BMD live to reproduce. Since males only transmit their Y chromosome to their sons, a man with BMD cannot pass the mutated dystrophin gene on the X chromosome to a male child. He can, however, transmit the mutant gene to a daughter, who will then be an MD carrier and can pass the MD gene to her sons. Doctors have reported cases of girls inheriting a recessive gene from a father with BMD and a mother who is a carrier, leading to very mild symptoms in the girl, but this is extremely unusual.

Emery-Dreifuss Muscular Dystrophy

Emery-Dreifuss muscular dystrophy can be X-linked recessive, autosomal dominant, or, rarely, autosomal recessive. The X-linked form of EDMD appears to be caused by a defect in the emerin gene that codes for the protein emerin. The defective gene prevents cells from producing this protein. The exact function of emerin has not yet been identified, but scientists do know that it is normally located in the membrane that sur-

Chromosome X

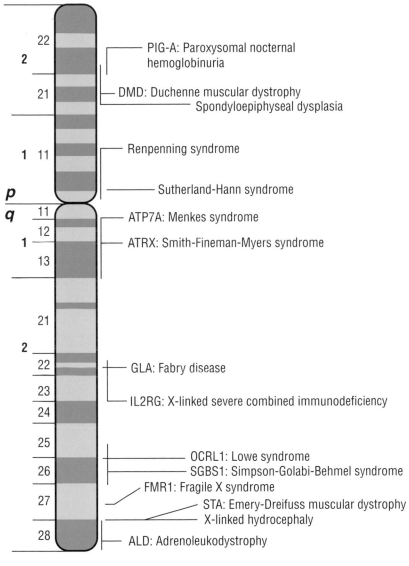

A diagram shows the regions of the X chromosome where genes tied to specific diseases and conditions are located, including the Duchenne and Emery-Dreifuss types of muscular dystrophy.

rounds each cell's nucleus and is important for the normal function of heart and skeletal muscles.

The autosomal dominant and recessive forms of EDMD are caused by mutations in the LMNA (lamin A/C) gene that codes for the proteins lamin A and lamin C. These proteins are found in the nuclear membrane, and their absence weakens the structure of the nucleus, making the cells more fragile.

Limb-Girdle Muscular Dystrophy

Different subtypes of limb-girdle muscular dystrophy are caused by a variety of genetic mutations. Six subtypes are autosomal dominant. The abnormal genes in autosomal dominant LGMD are on chromosomes 5, 6, or 7. They regulate the production of the proteins myotolin, caveolin, lamin A, or lamin C. These proteins are all needed for proper muscle function, and when a mutated gene causes any of them to be deficient, different symptoms of LGMD result. Mutations in the lamin A and C gene can also cause certain forms of EDMD, and doctors are not sure why some people with these mutations get LGMD and others get EDMD.

Eight different forms of autosomal recessive LGMD have been identified. These subtypes are caused by defects in genes that make the proteins sarcoglycans, dysferlin, calpain-3, telethonin, or TRIM32 (also known as tripartite motif-containing 32 or as zinc-finger protein HT2A). These proteins are necessary for maintaining the shape of muscle cell membranes or for allowing other parts of the cell to function properly. Without any one of them, the cell membrane or entire cell can break down. The various forms of autosomal recessive LGMD result from mutated genes on chromosomes 2, 13, 15, or 17.

The recessive subtypes of LGMD usually begin in childhood or adolescence, while the dominant subtypes begin in adulthood. About 90 percent of people with LGMD have one of the recessive forms.

Some doctors refer to the subtypes of LGMD by letters and numbers that symbolize whether the disorder is dominant or recessive and which particular gene is involved. For example,

Discovery of the Dystrophin Gene Mutation

Dr. Louis M. Kunkel and his associates at Children's Hospital in Boston discovered the dystrophin gene in 1986. First, they identified the region of the X chromosome where the gene was located by taking muscle cells from several DMD patients and chemically staining those cells so the chromosomes were visible under a microscope. After analyzing abnormalities in the X chromosome, they concluded that the mutant gene was in the middle of the short arm. Each chromosome in a cell is naturally divided into two sections by a structure called a centromere. The shorter section is known as the short arm and the longer section as the long arm.

Once they identified the region, Kunkel and his colleagues performed linkage studies to establish the gene's precise location. In linkage studies, scientists stain the chromosomes of many patients who have a particular disease to reveal common abnormalities in the bands that are visible on each chromosome. A particular abnormal band can then be "linked" to that disease, and the location of a gene pinpointed to that band. The dystrophin gene is located at Xp21. X identifies the chromosome, p stands for the short arm, and 21 is the number of the band, as measured by its distance from the centromere.

LGMD1A refers to an autosomal dominant form that involves the myotolin gene. LGMD2A is an autosomal recessive subtype that is caused by defects in the calpain-3 gene. Other physicians and scientists classify the subtypes of LGMD according to the name of the deficient protein or gene. For instance, one subtype is known as alpha-sarcoglycan deficiency. Another is beta-sarcoglycan deficiency. The subtype that results from a deficiency in the calpain-3 protein is called calpainopathy.

The Muscular Dystrophy Association believes that doctors are increasingly referring to the specific LGMD subtype names rather than simply diagnosing patients with LGMD. "In the future, the term *limb-girdle muscular dystrophy* may become obsolete and be replaced by more specific terms."[23]

Facioscapulohumeral Muscular Dystrophy

Facioscapulohumeral muscular dystrophy is inherited as an autosomal dominant trait. The mutation is on chromosome 4, where a shorter than normal segment of DNA causes the disease. The larger the piece of missing DNA, the more severe is the case of FSHMD. Researchers at the University of Massachusetts Medical School in Worcester believe that the missing DNA segment, called D4Z4, fails to suppress a gene known as FRG1 (FSHD region gene 1), and when this gene is not deactivated, FSHMD results. As the Muscular Dystrophy Association explains:

> When they [the researchers] analyzed genetically altered mice that produced low, medium, or high levels of the FRG1 protein, they found that the higher the FRG1 levels were, the worse the MD symptoms were in the mouse. Mice with elevated FRG1 levels showed spinal curvatures, muscle wasting (atrophy), increased connective tissue in the muscles, and reduced exercise tolerance, along with muscles that appeared dystrophic under the microscope.[24]

Distal Muscular Dystrophy

Distal muscular dystrophy is usually inherited as an autosomal dominant trait that begins to be apparent in people forty to sixty years of age, though sometimes it is caused by an autosomal recessive mutation that affects babies and young adults. Different genetic defects cause the various subtypes of DMD.

Welander Distal MD is caused by an autosomal dominant defect on chromosome 2. Scientists do not know which specific gene is responsible. Miyoshi distal myopathy is autosomal recessive and is caused by a defect in the gene for the dysferlin protein. Mutations in this gene also cause the subtype of limb-girdle MD known as LGMD2B, and doctors do not know why some patients with this genetic defect get LGMD2B and others get Miyoshi distal myopathy.

Finnish, or tibial, DD is caused by autosomal dominant mutations in the gene that makes the protein titin, which plays a role in muscle fiber structure and strength. Some people with this form of DD have one defective gene and experience mild weakness in muscles in the front of the calves. Others, who have two mutated genes, tend to develop the disease in childhood and lose the ability to walk.

Oculopharyngeal Muscular Dystrophy

Oculopharyngeal MD is usually autosomal dominant, though it can be autosomal recessive in rare cases. A mutation in the gene that codes for nuclear poly(A)-binding protein (PABPN1) is responsible for OPMD. When the gene for PABPN1 is defective, extra amino acids in the protein it produces cause the protein to clump in the muscle cells, trapping other proteins and RNA and disrupting the function of the cells. The defect in the PABPN1 gene that causes the extra amino acids to be produced is called a trinucleotide repeat expansion. Normally, the PABPN1 gene contains six consecutive repeats of the trinucleotide GCG (guanine, cytosine, guanine). People with OPMD, however, have eight to thirteen repeats. Scientists have found that the more repeats of this sequence a person with OPMD has, the more muscles are affected and the more severe is the disability.

Congenital Muscular Dystrophy

In the mid 1990s researchers found that about half of all cases of congenital muscular dystrophy result from a deficiency of the protein merosin. Merosin anchors muscle cells to the basal lamina, which is a coating that encases muscle cells. Depending on how much merosin is present, symptoms can range from mild to severe. These subtypes of CMD are referred to as merosin negative muscular dystrophies and are inherited as autosomal recessive traits due to a defective gene on chromosome 6.

In 1998 investigators identified another mutation that causes several other forms of CMD. This is in the gene for integrin, a substance that surrounds and protects each muscle fiber and connects merosin to proteins inside muscle cells. The gene is on chromosome 12 and is autosomal recessive. People with this subtype of CMD are said to have integrin deficient CMD.

Another form of CMD called Ullrich CMD is caused by a lack of collagen 6, a protein that helps support muscle fibers. The lack of collagen 6 is caused by mutations on either chromosome 2 or 21. Collagen 6 normally connects to merosin, which in turn connects to either integrin or dystroglycan and then to muscle cells, so these proteins are all intertwined.

Dystroglycan connects the outer surface of muscle cells to structures inside the cells using branches made of sugar. If any of the proteins involved in making the sugar branches are defective or missing, this can lead to subtypes of CMD like Fukuyama CMD or Walker-Warburg syndrome. Fukuyama CMD is caused by an autosomal recessive mutation in the fukutin gene on chromosome 9. Walker-Warburg syndrome results from a lack of POMT1 (protein-O-mannosyltransferase1), POMT2, fukutin, or fukutin-related protein. These defects in turn result from mutations in genes on chromosomes 9, 14, or 19. POMT1, POMT2, fukutin, and fukutin-related protein are all important for the proper function of dystroglycan and for the manufacture of its sugar branches.

Scientists are investigating why similar mutations in certain genes and deficiencies in associated proteins can lead to different subtypes of CMD. They are still untangling the mysteries of how the specific proteins interact to maintain the integrity of muscle cells.

Myotonic Muscular Dystrophy

Most cases of myotonic muscular dystrophy are of the subtype MMD1. They are caused by autosomal dominant mutations on chromosome 19 that result in an abnormally long repetition of the trinucleotide CTG (cytosine, thymine, guanine) in a person's DNA sequence. Normally the CTG segment is repeated from five to thirty-five times, but the mutations cause it to repeat from fifty to five thousand times. The higher the number of repetitions, the worse is the case of MMD1. The repetition gets longer in each generation that inherits the disorder, and symptoms get accordingly worse. "This disease frequently increases in severity from one generation to the next, a phenomenon referred to as anticipation. Thus a grandfather with cataracts and mild myotonia may have a daughter with myotonia and muscle weakness who, in her turn, has a child with the serious congenital form of the disease,"[25] explains the author of *Muscular Dystrophy: The Facts.*

The elongated DNA that causes MMD1 occurs in the DMPK (dystrophia myotonica-protein kinase) gene that regulates myotonin protein kinase. Myotonin protein kinase is important for muscle contractions and for communication within muscle cells. The DMPK mutation causes the gene to produce abnormal messenger RNA. Messenger RNA translates DNA's genetic code into the amino acids that make up proteins. Researchers believe that the abnormal messenger RNA issues faulty instructions that lead to abnormal myotonin protein kinase.

The rarer subtype MMD2 is caused by an autosomal dominant mutation on chromosome 3. This mutation also involves an elongated section of DNA, this time in the CNPB (cellular nucleic acid binding protein) gene. The expanded portion of the gene can be repeated from seventy-five to eleven thousand times in people with MMD2. This leads the gene to produce abnormal messenger RNA that in turn produces proteins that clump in muscle cells.

CHAPTER FOUR

Living with Muscular Dystrophy

Living with muscular dystrophy is challenging from the time of diagnosis on. The diagnosis can produce different reactions in different people. Most are shocked, sad, and angry. Some parents whose children are diagnosed with MD blame themselves for passing on a genetic disease. As with other serious illnesses or life events, patients (if they are old enough to understand what is going on) and family members generally go through what is known as the coping process. Psychologists describe five stages in this coping process. Some people may get stuck in one of the stages indefinitely and never progress through all five stages.

The first stage is shock and denial. Here, an affected person and family may be so overwhelmed by the diagnosis that they deny it is true. Next comes the anxiety stage, where the diagnosis is accepted but anxiety about the future ensues. Experts say a patient and family should refrain from making important decisions about the future until this stage has passed. The anger and guilt stage follows the anxiety phase. Patients or family members may be angry at God, the physician, or themselves. Guilt over transmitting a genetic disease to a child often accompanies this anger. Then comes the depression stage, where affected parties fully understand the diagnosis and prognosis and become depressed about the reality of what is happening. In the next stage, the homeostasis phase, involved persons attempt to move past the negative feelings and move on with their lives, no matter how difficult things may be. Many people never reach this stage. Meghan, however, a single mother who has a son with DMD, did finally arrive at the homeostasis phase:

It took me years, literally, to fully understand what Zach and I were up against. I don't know when I finally gave in to the denial and the feelings of despair, but I did. It was not easy and there were so many ill directed emotions, however, I think a parent needs to experience the full range of feelings to be able to come out on the other side as a whole person. This is not to say that I do not get sad or get frustrated and wish for this 'thing' to go away, but I know that we will be together in our fight for a productive life together . . . Every time I see him smile or watch him conquer a task, I know that the fight is worth fighting.[26]

Support Systems

Psychologists encourage patients and families to talk about their feelings and thoughts at each stage of the coping process in order to gain acceptance of the situation. Sometimes talking to family members is sufficient, but often a mental health professional like a psychologist or psychiatrist is needed. Many people also find that attending support group meetings sponsored by a local hospital or Muscular Dystrophy Association chapter, or sharing experiences online with other affected people is helpful. "Recognizing that you are not alone may diminish the flood of strong emotions that inevitably accompany the diagnosis of muscular dystrophy. Feelings of separateness and isolation can be diminished by realizing that they have been experienced by many others and that understanding and constructive help are available,"[27] explains the author of *Muscular Dystrophy in Children: A Guide For Families*.

Furthermore, say experts at the Mayo Clinic, support groups and other types of networking can help patients and families

Participation in support groups is among the many ways that the families of people with muscular dystrophy learn to cope with the diagnosis and its effects.

cope well beyond the stages immediately following the diagnosis. "In dealing with a disease such as muscular dystrophy, support groups can be a valuable part of a wider network of social support that includes health care professionals, family, friends, and a place of religious worship . . . Support groups provide a setting in which people can share their common problems and provide ongoing support to one another."[28]

Ongoing Challenges

Even when constructive support is available, families face ongoing difficulties and decisions that can be stressful. For example, deciding whether to send a boy with Duchenne MD and scoliosis for back surgery can be a difficult decision for parents. On the one hand, the surgery has the potential to make the child more comfortable and to preserve lung function by removing pressure on the lungs exerted by a curved spine. On the other hand, surgery on the spine can be risky for even a person in good health and is riskier for someone with a chronic disease.

The reality of caring for a mobility-impaired patient may also cause a parent or other caretaker to feel isolated and over-worked. The caretaker of a child with MD may neglect other family members because of the sick child's needs. This can have a detrimental effect on relationships within the family. In many situations, however, having a disabled family member brings

---

Support Groups

Many MD patients and families find support groups to be helpful for problem solving, research updates, and emotional challenges, but some people are hesitant to attend local support groups or enter online support groups because they fear they will become depressed by others' problems. The Muscular Dystrophy Association, however, reports that support groups are generally a source of positive rather than negative life experiences: "Finding such support doesn't mean you'll find a room full of tears and sob stories. Sharing emotions is a priority, but so is exchanging ideas, victories and inspiration for living with neuromuscular disease. In fact, many participants find they receive the biggest boost by giving of themselves and sharing their tips for making life easier."

Brad, an LGMD patient who participates in an online chat support group, agrees that the group has a positive influence on him: "Not having any previous experience with support groups, I kind of had the vision that people would use it as an opportunity to bemoan their problems. Not so. The people in the chat groups have, for the most part, wonderful senses of humor, and we keep each other laughing a great deal."

1. Muscular Dystrophy Association, "MDA Support," 2006. www.mdausa.org/support-groups.html.
2. Quoted in Muscular Dystrophy Association, "Connecting the MDA Way," *Quest*, December 2000. www.mdausa.org/publications/Quest/q76connect.html.

the family closer together as they all do their part to help out. This is especially true when parents make time to show each of the children that he or she is loved and when they allow their other children to voice their concerns about the sick sibling. When the MD patient is an adult, experts recommend that the person assure his or her children that they will be taken care of if the parent dies. Also, children or teens should not be burdened with the primary responsibilities of being the parent's caretaker.

Whoever the primary caretaker may be, the author of *Muscular Dystrophy in Children: A Guide for Families* emphasizes that this person must not neglect his or her own well-being while attending to the patient's needs: "In muscular dystrophy the family is the patient. Caregivers have to care for themselves if they are going to continue helping their loved one to the best of their ability. It is important to arrange to give yourself a break by having a trained person take over your duties for a time."[29]

Facing Unique Challenges

Since many muscular dystrophy patients are children, they and their parents face unique challenges from the time of diagnosis on. One of the first important questions parents face is what and how much to tell the child about the illness. "With children it is probably not a good idea to discuss the full implications of the diagnosis at the very beginning. In many ways it is best to encourage questions and to answer them sensibly and honestly, in a way appropriate to the age and level of understanding. The best way is to provide a little information at a time and as often as questions and opportunities arise,"[30] advises MD expert Dr. Alan E.H. Emery in his book *Muscular Dystrophy: The Facts*. Emery also advises parents not to try to overprotect an affected child, but instead to allow the individual to function as fully as possible within the limits of his or her disability.

David, an adult who has had DMD since childhood, agrees that parents should not be overprotective of a child with MD: "I believe it is important for parents to treat their children with DMD like they would anyone else. I have witnessed parents

Despite having muscular dystrophy, Cub Scout Aaron Ruiz, center, collects donations for a canned food drive with the help of his sister and father. Many children with the disease benefit from enjoying the same activities as their peers.

who have harmed the character and growth of their children by being overprotective of them and sheltering them from the realities of life."[31]

Not being overprotective may include allowing a child with MD to play with nondisabled friends as much as possible and placing the child in a regular school. Some children with severe mental impairments or profound muscle weakness that prevents them from writing or eating may have to be placed in a special school for the disabled or may not be able to go to school at all. But many MD doctors say that if at all possible, a child who has MD should be encouraged to go to a mainstream school.

> Most boys with Duchenne muscular dystrophy whether intellectually compromised or not, derive most benefit from attending a normal school. Most teachers nowadays are sensitive to the particular needs of children with physical handicaps and there is much to be said for visiting the school beforehand in order to discuss the situation with the head teachers and their colleagues.[32]

While some children with MD feel more comfortable around disabled peers and prefer to attend a special school for the disabled, many do just fine in a mainstream setting, even when they are unable to walk, as Meghan, whose son Zach has DMD, explains:

> I see him in his new power scooter racing around the playground while his 'bi-pedal' classmates chase him shrieking and laughing in delight. I see how accepting his friends are of him and how accepting he is of their physical freedom. He puts them to work. If they can pick up something he has dropped or open a door for him, he will let them know. If his friends are too rowdy around him, he will state loud and clear that their behavior is way out of line for his needs. Zach will take charge and direct a crowd. What he lacks in physical mobility, he sure makes up vocally.[33]

Individuals with Disabilities in Education Act (IDEA)

Whether or not a child can attend a regular school, a federal law called the Individuals with Disabilities in Education Act (IDEA) mandates that disabled children up to age twenty-one be granted a free public education with appropriate accommodations for the disability. Officials must try to place disabled children in regular classrooms, but if this is not possible, the child is eligible for special education services in special classrooms or schools. Infants, toddlers, and preschool aged

Parenting a Child with Muscular Dystrophy

Parents who have a child with MD face heartbreak, uncertainty, and often isolation. A child with MD requires care for an assortment of medical and emotional problems.

In "Mastering Balance Beams: Parenting Children with Muscular Dystrophy," nurse and educator Joan Fleitas compares parenting a child with muscular dystrophy to walking on a balance beam:

> Have you ever walked on a balance beam? Much like a tightrope, the journey is perilous, with one step cautiously leading the other in an effort to remain stable atop the beam. Despite the winds—despite the narrowness of the beam—despite the distractions from below—the skill can be mastered. With persistence, much support, and an understanding that occasional falls might occur, "beam-walkers" can indeed be successful. Parenting children with muscular dystrophy is much like mastering balance beams.

Joan Fleitas, EdD, RN, "Mastering Balance Beams: Parenting Children with Muscular Dystrophy." www.parentprojectmd.org/site/PageServer?pagename=emo_fleitas_beams.

Children with muscular dystrophy are often able to attend school in regular classrooms, if accommodations are made for their disability.

children are also entitled to government-sponsored services provided in the child's home.

Any child eligible for services under IDEA is required to have an Individualized Education Program (IEP) formulated by the parents, teachers, and special education experts. The IEP is a document that specifies which services are required, how they will be implemented, and how progress will be assessed. Services can include special education assistance in a regular or special classroom, special transportation to and from school, speech and language therapy, physical and occupational therapy, and psychological counseling.

Before IDEA was implemented in 1975, only about 20 percent of children with physical and mental disabilities received public education. Many of the rest were either kept at home or housed in state institutions where they received little or no education. Some state laws prohibited children with certain types of disabilities from attending public schools. By 2006, over six million disabled children were enrolled in public education in the United States.

Although placing a child with MD in a public school setting can be a positive thing, sometimes it exposes him or her to stares, questions, or ridicule from other children or even from adults. This can also happen in any public setting such as a restaurant or store. Some children with MD and their parents choose to ignore such behavior, while others respond with a brief explanation about the disease to people who ask well-meaning questions. The important thing, MD experts say, is that the disabled child and parents learn to accept the child's condition and not let the reactions of strangers diminish their sense of self-worth.

Adolescents with Muscular Dystrophy

Adolescents with MD face many of the same educational and social challenges as affected children do, but during the teen years these challenges intensify as the individuals struggle to become adults while dealing with the day-to-day burden of a severe medical condition. "The [teen] with muscular dystrophy is faced with a difficult situation. His evolving weakness frustrates his attempts at physical independence. As his friends prepare for the challenges of life, including having a family and making vocational choices, the adolescent with DMD faces a life that offers fewer options and perhaps a limited life expectancy,"[34] writes the author of *Muscular Dystrophy in Children: A Guide for Families.*

Despite the hardships, some adolescents with MD lead extremely fulfilling lives and leave a lasting legacy to the world. Mattie Stepanek, for example, achieved international notoriety because of his upbeat attitude, motivational speeches about peace and tolerance, and five best selling "Heartsongs" poetry books. Mattie was also the national goodwill ambassador for the Muscular Dystrophy Association and won many awards for his advocacy for the disabled and for his poetry. He appeared on television shows such as the *Oprah Winfrey Show, Larry King Live, Good Morning America,* and the *Today Show* and

Mattie Stepanek served as National Goodwill Ambassador for the Muscular Dystrophy Association and gained international acclaim for his inspirational *Heartsongs* poetry books.

helped with the *Jerry Lewis Telethon* for years. He and singer Billy Gilman collaborated on a CD called "Music Through Heartsongs"; Mattie wrote the lyrics and Gilman sang. Mattie's philosophy, as quoted on his web site, was, "Remember to play after every storm."[35]

When Mattie died on June 22, 2004, at the age of thirteen, thousands of mourners attended his funeral services. Family, friends, celebrities, and other people who were touched by his life gathered to remember and honor this inspiring young man. Former U.S. president Jimmy Carter, who became one of Mattie's close friends, delivered the eulogy at the funeral. In his speech, Carter noted that in his many years of travel and of meeting heads of state all over the world, Mattie was "the most extraordinary person I ever met."[36]

Adults with Muscular Dystrophy

Like children and teens with MD, adults face many physical and emotional challenges. Some with the disease manage to work through feelings of anger and frustration and make the best of living with their disabilities, while others do not. One man with Becker MD, for instance, maintains a positive attitude and is married and employed. His brother, who also has Becker MD, resents the disease and remains isolated, depressed, and does not make an effort to lead as fulfilling a life as possible.

Increasing physical disability may make it impossible for some patients to hold a job even if they want to, but many adults with MD, especially those with the less severe forms, are able to work as long as the job is not physically demanding. Some teach, some are artists and writers, some are doctors. Many work in computer programming, diagnostics, graphics, or publishing. Even some with the most serious forms of muscular dystrophy like Duchenne MD surprise their physicians and families and live long enough to go to college and pursue a career, as Scott, a man in his forties, reveals:

When I was 18, I informed my doctor I'd be attending college in the fall. Later, he asked to speak to my parents

Adults with muscular dystrophy are assisted in their efforts to live productive, active lives when everyday tasks, such as using an ATM, are made easier through accessibility accommodations.

privately. He told them that, because I have Duchenne muscular dystrophy (DMD), they shouldn't expect me to survive to graduate. Well, I finished college. I'm now in my 40s and working as a software engineer . . . Most predictions are based on statistical averages and not absolute certainties. In fact, the most accurate prediction that can be made is that you and your family should be prepared for anything.[37]

For those who are not able to work or when the individual does not have medical insurance, financial difficulties often occur. This can also be true for families who have a child with MD. The expenses of day-to-day care, medical equipment and medication, and doctor and hospital bills can be substantial, even with medical insurance, which often does not cover all of the costs. Annual deductibles, copayments, transportation costs to get to specialized clinics, and other expenses can cost patients and families many thousands of dollars. Some people with no insurance and inadequate income are eligible to receive government assistance in the form of Medicaid or Supplemental Social Security Income, but some families who earn too much to qualify for these programs are unable to pay for their necessary medical care. Some patients take advantage of programs through organizations like the Muscular Dystrophy Association, which provides free medical equipment and access to specialized MD clinics throughout the United States. Some state governments send cash payments to parents who have disabled children.

End of Life Issues

As challenging as the many aspects of living with MD are, families say the greatest difficulties and heartbreak come when the patient approaches death. This is especially true when the patient is young, as the death of a child or teen is incredibly difficult for parents. Decisions on end of life care for patients of any age are painful and may include deciding whether or not to use invasive ventilation techniques, whether or not to try to resuscitate the patient if the heart stops, and whether to administer nourishment with a feeding tube if the patient becomes unconscious. Experts say it is best to discuss these issues in advance with doctors, family, and the patient present. The patient may want his or her desires formalized in a living will or advance medical directive, which is a document that specifies what measures should or should not be administered. An adult patient may also give a family member durable power of attorney that gives the person the legal right to make decisions for the patient if he or she is unable to communicate. In addition, the patient may specify a preference about where he or she wants to die, whether at home, in a hospital, or in a hospice (a care facility that specializes in helping terminal patients die with as much comfort and dignity as possible). Sometimes hospice workers will come to the patient's home to provide end of life care if the person prefers.

Prior to death, the emotions of the patient and family can run the gamut from denial to relief to sadness. The Muscular Dystrophy Association publication "Journey of Love" explains how different boys approaching the final stages of Duchenne muscular dystrophy may react: "Some young men in the later stages of DMD welcome the end of their struggle, while others insist on every last medical intervention that might give them a few more days or hours of life. Some are obsessed with the physical details of their experience, others crack jokes at every opportunity, and others want to verbalize their feelings about their lives and deaths."[38]

When the end finally comes, family members experience grief that they may live with for the rest of their lives. But many also find that the memories of how the loved one with MD enriched their lives stay with them forever. Margaret, whose son Mark died from an infection related to Duchenne MD, describes her experience:

> Harrowing, heartbreaking. There is no other way to tell the story. After 25 years I can still sob my heart out at the loss of my wonderful son, Mark . . . During the time we had Mark with us, I think we all learned something, that no one knows what is going to happen, no one knows how they will cope, and when a person you love dies, it is too late then to say "I love you". My children and I never part company, stop talking on the phone without first saying "I love you" as you never know if you will ever get the chance to say it again . . . Mark had a profound effect on all of us, he taught us patience, triumph over adversity, and to hold close to family—they are all you have in the final counting.[39]

CHAPTER FIVE

The Future

Since none of the existing therapies for muscular dystrophy actually halt progression of the disease, the lives of many patients are cut short after the person endures incapacitating disability. But scientists are testing some new treatments that have the potential to make life a lot better and longer. A great deal of research is being conducted in areas like gene therapy, stem cell transplants, new drugs, and new uses for existing drugs. In addition, investigators are making progress in further understanding the causes of the various forms of MD and in more accurately diagnosing these disorders. The research is being done throughout the world at many hospitals, clinics, university research centers, and government-funded institutes.

Developing and Testing Drugs

Currently, many drugs for MD are in various phases of testing. New drugs are originally invented and tested on animals in a laboratory. To test these drugs, scientists genetically engineer mice or other laboratory animals so they have a disease like human MD. They accomplish this by altering certain genes that cause different types of MD. Researchers refer to animals used in studies of human diseases as animal models.

Once a drug has been proven safe and effective in animal models, the drug developer may apply to the Food and Drug Administration (FDA) in the United States or to comparable agencies in other countries to begin testing on humans in clinical trials. A clinical trial generally involves three phases. Phase 1 lasts several months and is designed to determine safe doses, the best method of administering the drug, and tracking any adverse effects from the drug. Only a few patients, seldom more than twenty, participate in Phase 1 trials. All are volunteers who are informed that the drug being tested may or may not help them. People volunteer for clinical trials through physicians participating in the study or by contacting research centers that advertise the trials online.

When Phase 1 trials show that a drug appears to help people and is without side effects that outweigh the medication's benefits, Phase 2 may begin. Here, more volunteers, perhaps as many as one hundred, are given the drug to further test its safety and effectiveness. If the results of Phase 2 studies are satisfactory, Phase 3 follows. In Phase 3, which can last several

A scientist holds a mouse that has been genetically modified so that its muscles are resistant to the muscle wasting that would otherwise occur as it ages.

years, hundreds or even thousands of volunteers are randomly assigned to either experimental or control groups to test the drug's effectiveness. Patients in a control group are unknowingly given a placebo, or fake drug that looks like the real thing, so that scientists can assess whether expectations that a drug will work, rather than the actual drug itself, are responsible for any positive effects.

Once Phase 3 is completed satisfactorily, the FDA may approve the drug for marketing, and doctors may begin prescribing it for patients not included in the trials. Sometimes drug manufacturers then conduct Phase 4 studies that follow the drug's safety and effectiveness over many years.

New Drug Treatments Being Tested

Some drugs being tested for MD are designed to block a chemical in the body called myostatin, which inhibits muscle growth. Scientists hope that blocking myostatin will lead to muscle regeneration in animal models and people with MD. Several studies showed that the myostatin blocking antibody MYO-029, or stamulumab, led to muscle regeneration in mice. An antibody is a substance produced by the immune system to fight specific proteins such as bacteria or viruses. Scientists can create synthetic antibodies to fight infections or to inhibit chemicals in the body. MYO-029 is now being tested on humans with facioscapulohumeral MD, Becker MD, and limb-girdle MD in Phase 2 clinical trials.

A drug named ACVR2B also blocks myostatin and leads to dramatically increased muscle mass in mice. Se-Jin Lee of Johns Hopkins University in Baltimore, who is one of the researchers in the ACVR2B tests, says the effects of the drug were "larger and faster than we've seen with any other agent." However, he notes, ACVR2B acts on other chemicals besides myostatin. "The fact that this new inhibitor can block other [chemicals] in addition to myostatin is a potential down side of using this as a therapeutic, as the potential for side effects could be greater."[40]

Other investigators are attempting to improve muscle structure and function using a drug called poloxamer 188. This drug was tested in an experiment at the University of Michigan in Ann Arbor to see if it would strengthen heart muscle cells taken from mice with Duchenne MD. The treated cells showed normal resistance to stress delivered in the form of the drug dobutamine, which increases heart rate and blood pressure. Next, the researchers administered poloxamer 188 intravenously to mice with Duchenne MD and found that these animals did not experience heart failure when given dobutamine, unlike a group of Duchenne MD mice given dobutamine but not poloxamer 188. The scientists believe that poloxamer 188 repairs the fragile muscle cell membranes seen in muscular dystrophy. "If issues of dosing and long-term safety can be addressed, our results indicate that membrane-sealing poloxamers could represent a new class of therapeutic agents for heart muscle damage associated with DMD and possibly other types of MD involving defects in the muscle-cell membrane,"[41] they explain.

Testing Existing Drugs

Some studies seek to improve results with drugs that are already used to treat muscular dystrophy or with drugs approved to treat other illnesses. When existing drugs are tested for new uses or doses, researchers conduct clinical trials just as they would for gaining approval of a new medication. One study at Shriner's Hospitals for Children is testing whether different doses and frequencies of administration of the steroid cortisone helps boys with DMD walk better and longer while diminishing adverse side effects. Cortisone is currently used to slow down muscle degeneration in people with MD, but dangerous side effects make its use controversial.

Different types of steroids called anabolic steroids, usually used by body builders to bulk up muscles, are also being tested for use on people with MD. Although anabolic steroids can have serious side effects like kidney and liver damage, sterility, severe mood swings, and cancer, scientists are testing low doses of these drugs on boys with DMD. A recent Phase 1 clinical trial of oxandrolone, a synthetic anabolic steroid, showed that it slightly preserved muscle strength in these boys. Doctors are hoping to test a combination of anabolic steroids and other drugs to try to slow muscle degeneration even more.

HCT1026 is an anti-inflammatory drug approved for the treatment of arthritis. Recently, researchers in Milan, Italy, tested HCT1026 on mice with DMD and LGMD2D. They found that the drug reduced muscle inflammation and led to increased muscle strength. HCT1026 worked better than the steroid prednisolone and had none of the dangerous side effects.

A team of scientists at Johns Hopkins University tested the drug losartan, currently approved to treat high blood pressure, on DMD mice and found that muscles in the diaphragm showed less scarring than in untreated mice. The treated mice also had improved leg strength, less muscle fatigue, and more normal-appearing muscle fibers. The lead researcher in the losartan study believes that the drug has an excellent chance of helping people with DMD:

> We're very excited about the therapeutic potential of losartan for the treatment of people with Duchenne muscular dystrophy. First, it targets a process that appears to directly contribute to an important mechanism of disease—failure of muscle regeneration in response to injury. Second, it has proven remarkably effective in restoring and preserving muscle structure and function in a mouse model of Duchenne muscular dystrophy. The effects are substantial and enduring over the long haul in this mouse model. Finally, losartan is a safe medication that has been used extensively in the treatment of hypertension [high blood pressure] for nearly two decades.[42]

Genetic Research

Another area of intense research looks at defective genes that cause various types of MD. Since not all of the gene mutations responsible for certain types of MD have been identified, scientists are studying genetic material from MD patients and their families to try to locate faulty genes and the proteins they are supposed to make. Doctors at Children's Hospital in Boston who are conducting one such study explain the purpose of the research:

There are still many patients who have been identified for which no gene has been implicated in their disease. We feel that these patients may have genetic alterations in genes coding for dystrophin associated proteins which

Setbacks for Gene Therapy

Gene therapy has the potential to cure many genetic disorders such as MD. However, several tragic events have raised concerns about its safety. In one widely publicized case in 1999, a young man named Jesse Gelsinger received gene therapy for a rare genetic liver disease. Hours after doctors at the University of Pennsylvania injected copies of normal genes attached to viral vectors into his liver, Gelsinger developed a high fever, his blood began clotting and filling with toxic chemicals, and his immune system began attacking the injected material. He died four days later. After Gelsinger's death, the National Institutes of Health revealed that they had received reports of several hundred adverse reactions to gene therapy at other research centers. They began requiring new safety precautions for gene therapy research.

Other setbacks occurred in 2002 and 2003, when two children who received gene therapy to treat an immune system disorder developed leukemia, a deadly blood cancer. Doctors determined that the viral vectors used to transfer the healthy genes had inserted themselves next to cancer-causing genes in the children's cells and had activated the cancer-causing genes. Researchers had not been aware that an altered virus could activate deadly genes and are now more careful about using certain viral vectors.

we have yet to identify. Using molecular genetics to unravel the biochemical basis of these neuromuscular disorders should lead to more accurate diagnosis . . . and potential therapies.[43]

Researchers are also studying genes other than those that actually cause MD to see how these other genes affect the disease. For example, investigators at the University of Maryland School of Medicine found that an excess of the protein mu-crystallin exists in the muscles of people with FSHMD. This protein is produced by a gene on chromosome 16, whereas the genetic mutation that causes FSHMD is a deleted section of DNA on chromosome 4. The researchers believe that the excess mu-crystallin may contribute to some of the symptoms of FSHMD even though it does not directly cause the disorder.

Gene Therapy

An area of genetic research called gene therapy has the potential to cure many forms of MD by replacing mutated genes with normal ones. In gene therapy, doctors extract DNA from the cells of a healthy donor, isolate the appropriate gene from this DNA, and inject many copies of the healthy gene into an animal or person with a particular genetic defect. In the case of preparing a healthy gene to treat a patient with DMD or BMD, for example, the dystrophin gene would be isolated. Then a sequence of DNA called a promoter, which causes a gene to become active and synthesize a particular protein, would be added to the gene and the two cloned to produce millions of copies. The cloned gene and promoter would then be transferred to a patient or animal using a vector, or messenger. A vector is needed because if a gene and promoter are injected by themselves, they cannot easily penetrate the cells they are supposed to enter, and thus cannot start working properly. Scientists often use disabled viruses as vectors, since viruses very effectively enter cells (this is how they cause infections). Scientists prevent viral vectors from causing infections by removing some of their genetic material. They then attach the cloned

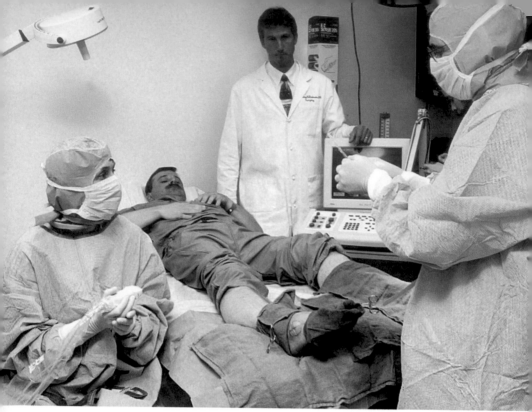

Doctors prepare Donovan Decker, second from left, who has limb-girdle muscular dystrophy, for the first gene therapy treatment for the disease in September 1999.

gene and promoter to the vector and inject the combination directly into a muscle or into the abdomen or bloodstream so it will spread throughout the body.

Many studies are testing gene therapy on mice and people with various forms of MD. One project at Columbus Children's Research Institute in Ohio is testing the safety and effectiveness of injecting the gene for alpha-sarcoglycan into the muscles of patients with LGMD2D (a subtype of limb-girdle MD). The investigators plan to measure muscle strength and analyze muscle tissue using a muscle biopsy ninety days after injection and at subsequent annual assessments.

Researchers at McGill University in Montreal, Canada, are studying whether injecting genes for the protein utrophin into mice with DMD will improve symptoms and delay progression of the disease. Utrophin is similar to dystrophin, the protein that is missing in DMD. Utrophin is not deficient in DMD, but scientists have found that if they increase the amount of utrophin in muscle cells, this protein can take over the functions of dystrophin.

Explaining why it would be preferable to transfer utrophin genes rather than normal dystrophin genes into people with DMD, the Muscular Dystrophy Association says, "The advantage to injecting utrophin instead of dystrophin genes is that the immune systems of at least some children and adolescents may reject the new dystrophin as a foreign protein, while they will almost certainly accept extra utrophin, since people with DMD already make utrophin."[44] In the study at McGill University, injecting extra utrophin genes into the leg muscles of DMD mice resulted in increased levels of utrophin, increased muscle strength, and better resistance to muscle damage. However, these effects lasted only a few months to a year after injection. The researchers have suggested that perhaps utrophin gene therapy coupled with the administration of a chemical that increases utrophin production from utrophin genes already in the body would lead to improved results. Other scientists are looking for chemicals that can achieve this function.

Repairing Gene Mutations

While gene transfer techniques involve replacing faulty genes with normal ones or adding extra normal genes to increase production of desired proteins, a different type of genetic research aims to repair gene mutations by inducing cells to skip over specific errors in the defective gene when they read the gene's instructions. Compounds used to achieve this are called exon skipping compounds. "Exons are regions of a gene that contain portions of the code, or recipe, for a protein,"[45] explains an article in the MDA publication *Quest*. Scientists believe that exon skipping is easier to accomplish than gene transfer because it is technically less complicated and less expensive to manufacture the necessary exon skipping chemicals than it is to prepare healthy genes within a viral vector.

Some chemicals used to induce exon skipping are called antisense oligonucleotides. Antisense oligonucleotides are single strands of DNA or RNA that bind to and prevent specific abnormal nucleotides from making sense or being translated into defective proteins. In a Phase 1 trial at Imperial College London, researchers are injecting the antisense oligonucleotide called morpholino oligomer into the muscles of patients with DMD to see if this chemical will enable cells to bypass a mutation in the dystrophin gene and to thus produce dystrophin. This technique has already been successful in cultured human DMD muscle cells and in experiments on mice and dogs with DMD.

Exon skipping compounds are designed to work only on specific gene mutations, so they would only help MD patients whose exact mutations were known. In one current project, Dutch researchers at Leiden University are injecting exon skipping compounds targeted to DMD patients who have missing exons numbered 48 to 52 in the dystrophin gene. Preliminary results of muscle biopsies showed that when injected into the lower legs, these chemicals led to the production of a shorter than normal, but usable, dystrophin protein in these muscles.

A technique known as stop codon read-through is similar to exon skipping. Stop codons are sequences of three nucleotides that direct cells to stop making a particular protein when the protein is complete. In mutated genes, however, the mutations may involve what is called a premature stop codon. A premature stop codon is an abnormal trinucleotide sequence that tells cells to stop making a protein before the protein is complete. For example, about 10 percent of cases of DMD are caused by a premature stop codon in the dystrophin gene. Certain antibiotics like gentamicin have been found to cause cells to ignore premature stop codons in mice with this form of DMD, thereby allowing the cells to read the gene's instructions and to produce dystrophin. However, this drug will only help those animals or people with this particular premature stop codon. Others with DMD whose dystrophin gene mutations result from other sorts of trinucleotide defects would see no benefit. Gentamicin can also cause hearing loss and kidney damage, so doctors must be careful when administering the drug.

Controversy over Stem Cell Research

Research progress on stem cells, which have the potential to replace diseased muscle cells in cases of muscular dystrophy and other types of cells in other diseases, has been slow because the subject has become a political as well as a scientific issue. On August 9, 2001, President George W. Bush signed legislation restricting federal funding of embryonic stem cell research to stem cell lines already taken from human embryos. Behind this legislation was the belief that taking stem cells from embryos destroys a life that could have matured into a human being. Opponents of this view believe that the potential for curing many devastating illnesses with stem cells outweighs the disadvantages of destroying embryos that would have been destroyed anyway. Embryos used in stem cell research are extras made and stored in a laboratory for use in impregnating infertile women. Since they are extras, however, they would simply be destroyed if they were not used as sources of stem cells for research. This has led many scientists and advocates of embryonic stem cell research to argue that the Bush administration policy should be changed.

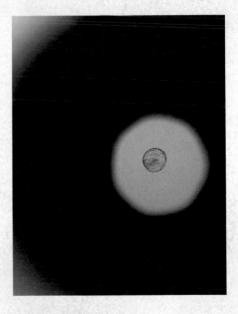

A microscope reveals a human embryo, which is a key but controversial source of stem cells used in medical research.

PTC124, another drug that causes cells to ignore premature stop codons, seems safer than gentamicin. Researchers at the University of Pennsylvania found that DMD mice fed and/or injected with PTC124 showed less muscle damage and became stronger than untreated mice. Blood tests revealed that levels of creatine kinase also decreased. This meant that muscle cells were not leaking as much creatine kinase into the bloodstream. PTC124 caused no toxic effects, and it acted only on the mutated dystrophin genes and did not interfere with the function of other genes. Scientists at several medical centers have begun human trials of PTC124. Muscle biopsies on boys with DMD given PTC124 by mouth for nearly one month showed increased levels of dystrophin. Blood tests showed reduced levels of creatine kinase. Some patients also experienced improved muscle strength.

Stem Cell Transplants

Another area of high-tech research involves efforts to repopulate diseased muscles with healthy cells by transplanting stem cells into the muscles. Stem cells, also called precursor cells, can develop into any type of cell in the body, depending on the biochemical instructions they are given. They can be harvested from embryos, or, in lesser quantities, from adult donors. The immune system of someone who receives adult stem cells may reject the transplanted cells and destroy them, but rejection does not occur when embryonic stem cells are used in transplants. However, controversy over the morality of using cells taken from human embryos has led to reduced federal funding for embryonic stem cell research, and scientists are exploring techniques of making transplanted adult stem cells more viable.

A problem with stem cell transplantation that researchers are addressing is that sometimes the injected cells do not multiply enough to fuse to existing muscle fibers or to form new fibers. Conversely, in some studies, transplanted stem cells multiply too much and turn cancerous. In one study where stem cells taken from healthy adult mice were injected into mice with MD,

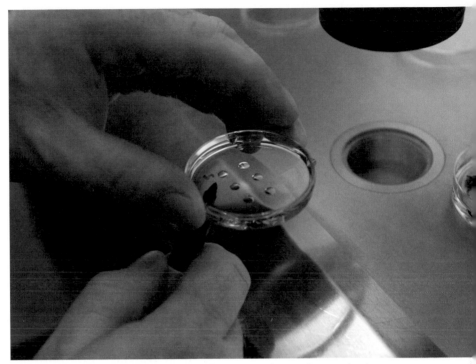

A scientist holds a dish containing human embryos from which stem cells can be harvested for research or medical use. Researchers are learning how to best transplant stem cells into diseased muscles in order to help people with muscular dystrophy.

for example, the cells replicated themselves up to three hundred times in six months. This rapid growth resulted in some of the cells turning into cancer cells. The National Institute of Arthritis and Musculoskeletal and Skin Diseases cautions that such dangers must be resolved: "The potential of highly expanded muscle stem cells to become cancerous [means that] the biological behaviors of stem cells need to be further studied."[46]

One group of researchers at Laval University in Quebec City, Canada, is getting around the problem of rejection of adult stem cells by giving patients drugs that suppress the immune system. However, these drugs also diminish the body's ability to fight infections, so doctors must be very careful about prescribing them. The Laval scientists are also trying to circumvent the problem of precursor cells not spreading after injection by using a technique called high-density cell transplantation. Here, millions of stem cells are injected at one time. Preliminary results showed that muscle fibers in DMD patients given high-density transplants began making dystrophin. It remains to be seen whether these patients will experience improvements in muscle function.

Other research on stem cells at Children's Hospital of Pittsburgh, the University of Pittsburgh, and the University of California Los Angeles found that stem cells taken from the muscles of healthy female mice and transplanted into mice with MD fused more readily with existing muscle fibers and caused these fibers to regenerate better than did stem cells taken from healthy male mice. The investigators believe this occurred because stem cells from females stay immature longer than those from males. While male stem cells mature into muscle cells immediately after transplant, female stem cells do not mature for about three days. This time lapse allows any inflammation from the transplant to heal, thereby giving the stem cells more oxygen to help them regenerate muscle fibers. This type of research can help scientists develop more efficient and safe ways of successfully transplanting stem cells that may improve the condition of many people with various types of muscular dystrophy.

The Goal of Muscular Dystrophy Research

The goal of all this research is to improve the quality and length of life for people with MD and eventually to develop ways of preventing and curing these diseases. As stated by the National Institute of Neurological Disorders and Stroke, "Past research has led to the discovery of disease mechanisms and improved treatment for many forms of MD. Current research promises to generate further improvements. In the coming years, physicians and patients can look forward to new forms of therapy developed through an understanding of the unique traits of MD."[47]

Notes

Introduction: Jerry Lewis and the Muscular Dystrophy Association Telethon

1. Muscular Dystrophy Association, "MDA Telethon," 2006. www.mda.org/telethon/faqs.html.
2. Muscular Dystrophy Association, "MDA Summer Camp," 2006. www.mda.org/clinics/camp/.
3. Quoted in Jerry Lewis Comedy, "Jerry Lewis Biography." www.jerrylewiscomedy.com/biography.htm.
4. Quoted in "Jerry Lewis Criticized over Telethon's Approach," *New York Times*, September 6, 1992. http://query.nytimes.com/gst/fullpage.html?res=9E0CE0DC143E F935A3575AC0A964958260&scp=1&sq=Jerry+Lewis+Criti cized+over+Telethon%27s+approach&st=nyt.
5. The Kids Are All Right, "About The Film," 2005. http://thekidsareallright.org/about.php?PHPSESSID=1580f3a64f d50bb50db28cf6fbe39078.
6. Muscular Dystrophy Association, "MDA Telethon."

Chapter 1: What is Muscular Dystrophy?

7. National Institute of Neurological Disorders and Stroke, "Muscular Dystrophy: Hope Through Research," February 12, 2008. www.ninds.nih.gov/disorders/md/detail_md.htm.
8. National Institute of Neurological Disorders and Stroke, "NINDS Muscular Dystrophy Information Page," February 12, 2008. www.ninds.nih.gov/disorders/md/md.htm.
9. Quoted in Parent Project Muscular Dystrophy, "Lyndsey's Story." www.parentprojectmd.org/site/PageServer?pagename=emo_stories.
10. Muscular Dystrophy Association, "Emery-Dreifuss Muscular Dystrophy," www.mda.org/publications/fa-rareMD.html.
11. Quoted in Margaret Wahl, "Matters of the Heart: Cardiac Problems Take Center Stage in Emery-Dreifuss MD,"

Quest, May–June 2005. www.mda.org/publications/Quest/q123edmd.html.

12. Muscular Dystrophy Association, "Facts About Limb-Girdle Muscular Dystrophy," October 2007. www.mda.org/publications/fa-lgmd-qa.html.

13. Alan E.H. Emery, *Muscular Dystrophy: The Facts*. New York: Oxford University Press, 2000, p. 40.

14. Muscular Dystrophy Association, "Congenital Muscular Dystrophy," December 2006. www.mda.org/publications/fa-rareMD.html.

Chapter 2: Diagnosis and Treatment

15. National Institute of Neurological Disorders and Stroke, "Muscular Dystrophy: Hope Through Research."

16. Parent Project Muscular Dystrophy, "Frequently Asked Questions About Wheelchairs," 2003. www.parent-projectmd.org/site/PageServer?pagename=tc_wheelchairsfaq.

17. Emery, *Muscular Dystrophy: The Facts*, p. 57.

18. Muscular Dystrophy Association, "Facts About Duchenne and Becker Muscular Dystrophies (DMD and BMD)," 2006. www.mda.org/publications/fa-dmdbmd-treat.html.

19. Muscular Dystrophy Association, "Facts About Duchenne and Becker Muscular Dystrophies (DMD and BMD)."

Chapter 3: What Causes Muscular Dystrophy?

20. Emery, *Muscular Dystrophy: The Facts*, p. 6.

21. Muscular Dystrophy Association, "Genetics and Neuromuscular Disease," November 2007. www.mda.org/publications/gen_faq.html.

22. Muscular Dystrophy Association, "Facts About Duchenne and Becker Muscular Dystrophies (DMD and BMD)."

23. Muscular Dystrophy Association, "Facts About Limb-Girdle Muscular Dystrophy."

24. Muscular Dystrophy Association, "Scientists ID Molecular Consequences of FSHD Mutation," March 20, 2006. www.mdausa.org/research/060320fshd_frg1.html.

25. Emery, *Muscular Dystrophy: The Facts*, p. 45.

Chapter 4: Living with Muscular Dystrophy

26. Quoted in Parent Project Muscular Dystrophy, "Meghan's Story." www.parentprojectmd.org/site/ PageServer?pagename=emo_stories.
27. Irwin M. Siegel, MD, *Muscular Dystrophy in Children: A Guide for Families*. New York: Demos, 1999, p. 98.
28. Mayo Clinic, "Muscular Dystrophy," December 8, 2007. www.mayoclinic.com/health/muscular-dystrophy/ DS00200/DSECTION=7.
29. Siegel, *Muscular Dystrophy in Children: A Guide for Families*, p. 92.
30. Emery, *Muscular Dystrophy: The Facts*, p. 75.
31. Quoted in Parent Project Muscular Dystrophy, "David's Story." www.parentprojectmd.org/site/ PageServer?pagename=emo_stories.
32. Emery, *Muscular Dystrophy: The Facts*, p. 92.
33. Quoted in Parent Project Muscular Dystrophy, "Meghan's Story."
34. Siegel, *Muscular Dystrophy in Children: A Guide for Families*, pp. 59-60.
35. Quoted in Mattie Online, "About Mattie Stepanek," 2005. www.mattieonline.com/about.htm.
36. Quoted in Tara Wood "Memories, Jokes and Respect Mark Mattie's Services," *MDA.org*, June 28, 2004. www. mda.org/mattie/.
37. Quoted in Muscular Dystrophy Association, "Learning to Live with Neuromuscular Disease: A Message for Parents," April 2006. www.mda.org/publications/learning/ neuro.html.
38. Muscular Dystrophy Association, "Journey of Love," 1998. www.mda.org/publications/journey/10.html.
39. Quoted in Parent Project Muscular Dystrophy, "Margaret's Story." www.parentprojectmd.org/site/ PageServer?pagename=emo_stories.

Chapter 5: The Future

40. Quoted in Muscular Dystrophy Association, "New Myostatin Blocker Makes Mouse Muscles 60 Percent Larger," January 6, 2006. www.mda.org/

research/060106myostatin_blocker.html.

41. Quoted in Muscular Dystrophy Association, "Research Updates," November/December 2005. www.mda.org/publications/Quest/q126resup.html#dmd_damage.

42. Quoted in Muscular Dystrophy Association, "Two Anti-Fibrosis Drugs Show Promise in Mice with DMD," February 6, 2007. www.mda.org/research/070206dmd_anti_fibrosis.html.

43. National Institutes of Health, "Molecular Analysis of Patients with Neuromuscular Disease," July 2007. clinicaltrials.gov/ct/show/NCT00390104;jsessionid=9527DA40992E16BDAD4D726559134FA2?order=1.

44. Muscular Dystrophy Association, "Utrophin Gene Therapy Benefits DMD Mice," August 17, 2007. www.mda.org/research/070817dmd-mice-utrophin.html.

45. Margaret Wahl, "Tackling DMD on Many Fronts," *Quest*, July 2007, p. 14. http://www.mdaquest-digital.com/mdaquest/20070708/?pg=14.

46. National Institute of Arthritis and Musculoskeletal and Skin Diseases, "Adult Mouse Stem Cells Are Capable of Long-Term Self-Renewal," May 2006. http://www.niams.nih.gov/News_and_Events/Spotlight_on_Research/2006/adult_stem_renew.asp.

47. National Institute of Neurological Disorders and Stroke, "Muscular Dystrophy: Hope Through Research."

Glossary

arrhythmia: Abnormal heart rate.

autosome: A chromosome that is not sex-linked.

cardiomyopathy: Weakness of the heart muscle.

chromosome: A worm-shaped body in the nucleus of each cell on which genes reside.

codon: A sequence of three adjacent bases, or chemical building blocks, on a strand of DNA or RNA that provides genetic instructions for a particular protein.

contracture: Chronic tightness of muscles or tendons around joints.

creatine kinase: A protein needed for muscle contractions.

dominant gene: A gene that leads to a particular trait when only one such gene is inherited.

exon: Region of a gene that contains portions of the code for a particular protein.

gene: The part of a DNA molecule that transmits hereditary information.

muscular dystrophy: A group of diseases that involve progressive muscle weakness in various parts of the body.

nucleotides: Short DNA sequences that comprise the building blocks for genes.

recessive gene: A gene that leads to a particular trait only when inherited from both parents.

Organizations to Contact

Facioscapulohumeral Muscular Dystrophy (FSHD) Society
3 Westwood Road
Lexington, MA 02420
Phone 781-275-7781 or 781-860-0501
Fax 781-860-0599
www.fshsociety.org

Provides information on facioscapulohumeral muscular dystrophy.

International Myotonic Dystrophy Organization
P.O. Box 1121
Sunland, CA 91041-1121
Phone 818-951-2311 or toll-free 866-679-7954
www.myotonicdystrophy.org

Provides information and support for people with myotonic dystrophy and their families.

Muscular Dystrophy Association
3300 East Sunrise Drive
Tucson, AZ 85718-3208
Phone 520-529-2000 or toll-free 800-344-4863
Fax 520-529-5300
www.mda.org

Provides general information on the muscular dystrophies, research support, and links to support groups.

Muscular Dystrophy Family Foundation

3951 N. Meridian Street, Suite 100
Indianapolis, IN 46208-4062
Phone 317-923-6333 or toll-free 800-544-1213
Fax 317-923-6334
www.mdff.org

Provides support services and funds adaptive equipment for patients.

National Institute of Arthritis and Musculoskeletal and Skin Diseases (NIAMS)

National Institutes of Health DHHS
31 Center Drive, Room 4C02 MSC 2350
Bethesda, MD 20892-2350
Phone 301-496-8190 or toll-free 877-226-4267
www.niams.nih.gov

Supports and conducts research on muscular dystrophy and provides general information on these diseases.

National Institute of Neurological Disorders and Stroke (NINDS)

NIH Neurological Institute
P.O. Box 5801
Bethesda, MD 20824
Phone 301-496-5751 or toll-free 800-352-9424
www.ninds.nih.gov

Provides general information and funds and conducts research.

Parent Project Muscular Dystrophy

1012 North University Boulevard
Middletown, OH 45042
Phone 513-424-0696 or toll-free 800-714-5437
Fax 513-425-9907
www.parentprojectmd.org

Provides information and advocacy on Duchenne and Becker muscular dystrophies.

For Further Reading

Books

Thomas Bergman, *Precious Time: Children Living with Muscular Dystrophy (Don't Turn Away)*. Milwaukee, WI: Gareth Stevens, 1996. Describes the life of a boy with Duchenne muscular dystrophy.

Miriam Kaufman, *Easy for You to Say: Q&A's for Teens Living with Chronic Illness Or Disability*. Buffalo, NY: Firefly, 2005. Written for teens with a variety of chronic illnesses and disabilities, including a section on muscular dystrophy.

Web Sites

Joan Fleitas, EdD, RN, "Mastering Balance Beams: Parenting Children with Muscular Dystrophy." www.parentprojectmd.org/site/PageServer?pagename=emo_fleitas_beams. Article provides insight into the challenges faced by parents of children with muscular dystrophy.

National Institute of Neurological Disorders and Stroke, "Muscular Dystrophy: Hope Through Research." www.ninds.nih.gov/disorders/md/detail_md.htm. Easily understood sections on history, types of MD, causes, diagnosis, treatment, and research.

Nemours Foundation, "Muscular Dystrophy." www.kidshealth.org/teen/diseases_conditions/bones/muscular_dystrophy.html. Health site targeted to teens provides an overview of types of muscular dystrophy, diagnosis, treatment, and living with the disease.

Tara Wood, "Memories, Jokes and Respect Mark Mattie's Services." www.mdausa.org/mattie/. A tribute to Mattie Stepanek's inspiring life and meaningful memorial services.

Index

Picture Credits

Cover: © Thomas Hansson/Big Stock Photo.com
© Ann Johansson/Corbis, 48
ALIX/PHANIE/Photo Researchers, Inc., 68
ALIX/Photo Reseachers, Inc., 36
AP Images, 12, 65, 82
© Bettmann/Corbis, 17
Biophoto Associates/Photo Researchers, Inc., 46
Custom Medical Stock Photo, Inc. Reproduced by permission, 28, 62
Gale, Cengage Learning, 16, 24, 51, 53
James King-Holmes/Photo Researchers, Inc., 50
© Ed Kashi/Corbis, 72
National Library of Mcdicine/Photo Researchers, Inc., 19
© Richard T. Nowitz/Corbis, 37
Reproduced by permission of the Muscular Dystrophy Association, 10, 70
© Reuters/Corbis, 76
Sandy Huffaker/Getty Images, 85, 87
Simon Fraser/Photo Researchers, Inc., 34
Simon Fraser/Royal Victoria Infirmary/Photo Researchers, Inc., 39
SMC Images/The Image Bank/Getty Images, 42
VEM/Photo Researchers, Inc., 31

About the Author

Melissa Abramovitz grew up in San Diego, California, and as a teenager developed an interest in medical topics. She began college with the intention of becoming a doctor but later switched majors, graduating summa cum laude from the University of California, San Diego, with a degree in psychology in 1976.

Launching her career as a writer in 1986 to allow herself to be an at-home mom when her two children were small, she realized she had found her niche. She continues to write regularly for magazines and educational book publishers and has published hundreds of articles and numerous short stories, poems, and books for children, teens, and adults. Many of her works are on medical topics.